WOMEN AND GIRLS' CRICKET

First published in 2023 by Sequoia Books

ISBN
Print: 9781914110160
EPUB: 9781914110177

A CIP record for this book is available from the British Library

Library of Congress Cataloguing-In-Publication Data

Name: Lydia Greenway
Title: Women and Girls Cricket / Lydia Greenway
Description: 1st Edition, Sequoia Books UK 2023
Subjects: LCSH:. Women in Sports, Sports
Print: 9781914110160
EPUB: 9781914110177

Library of Congress Control Number: 2022922457

Print and Electronic production managed by Deanta Global

WOMEN AND GIRLS' CRICKET
HOW WE CAN GROW THE GAME TOGETHER

Lydia Greenway

SEQUOIA
B O O K S

Contents

Foreword   vi

1   Introduction: Why Women's and Girls' Cricket?   1

2   How to Develop a Successful Club or School Programme   22

3   Coaching Female Cricketers and Teams   48

4   How to Develop Mentally Strong Cricketers   70

5   Formats, Techniques and Tactics   95

6   Practical Games, Drills and Coaching Tips   118

7   Selecting and Using the Right Kit   134

8   Equality, Diversity and Inclusion   143

9   Advice for Players   160

Glossary of Terms   171

Foreword

Women's cricket today is unrecognisable from when I retired in 2006. Quite simply, at every level, it is a sport transformed. This is in large part thanks to thousands of energetic people *working together* towards an inspiring goal – the goal of growing the game for women and girls so that they can have the same opportunities as men and boys have had for decades.

Throughout this book, you'll read about the vast improvements to the game across the world. Here in England, we've become a true high-performance sport with our national performance base at Loughborough, giving us access to coaching, sport science and everything a female player needs to fulfil her potential.

The main area of focus now is around professionalising the domestic game. When Lydia and I were playing, the women's domestic environment was entirely amateur.

When I look back in 30 years' time, I'll see the Kia Super League (KSL) as one of the breakthrough moments in the growth of the game in England. The KSL showed that the women's domestic game was ready to take that step into a more professional era and to do things differently to thrive.

Now, we're building a full-time professional women's domestic structure with eight teams. We have The Hundred, inclusion in the Commonwealth games, the Women's IPL on the horizon and so many more competitions that are providing women cricketers with the platform to show the world what they can do.

Who could have imagined the immediate impact The Hundred has made on the women's game? We all had high hopes for it, but it has been overwhelming to witness the quality of cricket, record TV viewing figures and hundreds of thousands of young, diverse fans clamouring to watch it live in the venues.

Across the competition, over eight million people tuned in to watch domestic women's cricket, the majority for the first time, alongside a total attendance figure of 267,000. A truly transformational level of reach, scale and profile, providing a big stage to match the increasing levels of professionalism being put in place for the women's game both on and off the field.

High-performance infrastructure, better remuneration, the frequency of global tournaments, the opportunities for all ages to play and the profile of the game have all improved enormously in this time. Similarly, we have seen a greater diversity of women involved in the sport. One example of this is that we now have nearly 2,000 South Asian female volunteers involved in the Dream Big programme. It's so exciting for diverse communities to have female role models in cricket, enabling girls and young women to feel safe and welcomed.

But yet we're not even close to being where we need and want to be as a fully inclusive, gender-equal sport. There's an awful lot of work to do, and we won't get there unless we *work together*. So now it's time to build on that success with even greater determination.

The growth of the grassroots game with All Stars and Dynamos in England has been wonderful, with almost 30% of participants now female. It's now in recreational cricket clubs where we need to double down and show the same focus.

Cricket clubs at a local level present multifaceted challenges reliant as they are on volunteers, facilities, pitches, committees, coaching and a culture that has historically been heavily male.

It's actually more straightforward to launch The Hundred or All Stars and Dynamos, as these are new national initiatives, created from inception for men and women, boys and girls, and can be centrally coordinated by the National Governing Body. However, progress across cricket clubs requires dedicated support from volunteers to do the hard work for their communities. Many are doing remarkable things for women and girls, but there is still so much more to be done at this level of our game. I sincerely hope that this book will make a valuable contribution to those curious about what they can do to help.

It's going to take some very energetic *men and women* who not only care about equal opportunity in cricket but who also understand the business case for change. Clubs invariably want more members, more volunteers, more funds and more community engagement. The women's and girls' game is the best route to achieve all of this, and so much more. A club should be a place for *everyone* in the community to gather and thrive.

Cricket truly is the ultimate team sport that can help set players up for life, from all backgrounds. It has everything a team sport can possibly provide: teamwork, leadership, a spirit of togetherness, resilience through adversity, joy, fun, health and countless other life skills. It has certainly provided all of that, and more, to me.

Cricket is a game that can and should be enjoyed by all. We're making great strides towards this vision, but we're not quite there yet. We'd love for you to come and join us on the journey. Thank you in advance for your support.

Clare Connor CBE, Head of England Women's Cricket at ECB and Former MCC President

CHAPTER 1

Introduction

Why Women's and Girls' Cricket?

Think of two separate images from the recent history of women's cricket.

Picture one: The Melbourne Cricket Ground in February 2008. Two of the best cricketing nations in the world playing in a T20 game. A young Ellyse Perry making her debut. England and Australia took to the field in front of a crowd of 27,000; you may think this is a lot, and it is, but most of these people had arrived early to get their seats for the men's game taking place after the women.

Picture two: The Melbourne Cricket Ground in March 2020. Two of the best cricketing nations in the world playing in a T20 World Cup Final – Australia and India – took to the field in front of 86,174 people to play each other in front of the biggest-ever crowd for a women's sporting event in Australia, the second largest crowd globally for a women's sporting event (first was the women's football World Cup Final between the United States and China in 1999 which saw 90,185 fans in attendance).

People had not arrived early to get their seats for the men's game – they had arrived early to see these brilliant women play. There was no men's game after them.

People were there to see players who had become household names.

Ellyse Perry, the youngster who made her T20 debut in 2008 sat on the sidelines injured to see her team take part in history and go on to beat India. There were over 1.1 billion video views across the world.

These two pictures are worlds apart, and so much has happened to have taken the game to where it is today – there has been a lot of hard work, but today is as good a day as any to be involved in the brilliant game of cricket if you are a female, not just at the elite level but across the board.

This chapter introduces us to how far women's cricket has come, the limitless potential it has to grow, why we should grow the game, how it can benefit schools and clubs, and how it can benefit the most important group of all, the females playing it.

The terms 'women' and 'girls' will be interchangeable throughout the book, but our intention is for the content to be applicable to females of all ages and abilities.

WHERE WE WERE AND WHERE WE ARE

Players of my generation, playing and learning in the 1990s, will have experienced a similar journey. More often than not they'd have been introduced to the game by a male relative and developed a passion for the game from there. I often wonder how many young girls during that time who loved sport but either didn't have that male relative or simply saw cricket as a boys' game were lost to the game. The opportunities from schools were almost non-existent; cricket clubs generally didn't have female teams, and the role models on TV from the professional game were exclusively male.

Insight: Heather Knight England Captain

I was once asked before a game, 'do you do the ironing for all your team after you finish playing?' I scored a 50 that day, that was quite nice.

For my generation, if we wanted to play, our only option was to play boys' cricket. In order to do this, you either had to be exceptionally good at cricket very quickly or have a great deal of confidence and resilience to play in an environment outside of your usual peer group. We'd turn up to the ground and head to the changing rooms, where we'd then be asked to get changed in the toilet cubicle as there were never any female changing areas. The attitudes to girls playing in boys' team were often quite 'old school'. People didn't necessarily think girls should be playing in a boys' team; this might include parents of the opposition teams, coaches or umpires and was just one of many things that girls had to contend with.

Insight: Jodie Hawkins, Sports Administrator

At the time of writing, The BBL* salary cap is $1.9 mil. The WBBL* salary cap for the exact same amount of games and you'd argue almost the same amount of training is $310,000. So there's not equality there. We talk about equality of pay in hours trained but I even think that's bull to be brutally honest. So, we're still not there in our own country. But we're far enough ahead that we need to continue to be an example for other countries while continuing to invest here. Every time someone talks about putting more money in the BBL salary cap, I think why not put it in the WBBL salary cap? If you only knew. We've got some of the most marketable people in the country, in the world running around in our sports, and they're getting paid not even what the minimum contract of a men's BBL player or even grade cricketers. It just does my head in and it's why anything I've ever had control of, so training facilities, coaching staff, whatever I can control, it's same, same. Same access to wickets, same accommodation, same cars, same opportunities. It seems ridiculous to me that we can't find better parity. And the argument always comes back to, well, they're not making as much money.

Not yet.

But we need to invest in it to grow it. And then hopefully, one day that argument, I don't think it'll be in my lifetime or at least my sports administration lifetime, that we'll get to true parity.

I hope that conversation is almost dead by the time I'm done working in sport.

*Big Bash League and Women's Big Bash League are the professional domestic T20 competitions in Australia.

I see two kinds of girls playing the game today, those that really want to make it and want to be the best they can be, without being concerned about playing with boys or girls or being coached by men or women. The second type are those that aren't necessarily driven by making it to the elite levels; they simply love the game, they love the environment, they're with their friends and they love the social element of the game. For this second type of player, those opportunities were never there.

The culture at the time meant a young girl playing cricket was seen as an anomaly.

The picture nowadays is very different. The pathways into cricket have increased dramatically; girls are playing cricket in schools; clubs are actively setting up girls' teams where the environments and attitudes are so different from what they were. The ECB (England and Wales Cricket Board – The governing body of cricket in England and Wales) mixed-gender initiatives of *All Stars* and *Dynamos* for younger children are thriving, and we've seen full stadiums at the Melbourne Cricket Ground and Lord's for women's matches.

Insight: Henry Moeran, BBC Cricket Broadcaster and Producer

The advent of T20 cricket as a viable and popular version of the international game has, in my opinion, given women's cricket a huge boost. In the early days, the condensed format allowed for double headers with men's matches (a crucial opportunity to showcase the women's game) and also offer the opportunity for supporters to see a snapshot of the sport without the necessity of committing to a full day of 100 overs.

With T20 flourishing, the 2009–2016 T20 World Cups in England, Sri Lanka, Bangladesh and India were played alongside the men's tournaments giving players from around the world the added media exposure that could propel the game forward. The fact that from 2018 this tournament could become standalone with every game televised shows how this early exposure and publicity helped grow the game.

Conversely, we've also seen the old adage that sometimes to take two steps forward you must first take one back. The 2013 50-over World Cup in India – chaotically planned and marketed – served as a line in the sand for the women's game. The desire for professionally played and broadcast international sport was at odds with a tournament that with a week until the first ball was bowled was uncertain to go ahead. The media uproar and fan frustration no doubt alerted the ICC and governing bodies around the world that the women's game could no longer be an afterthought.

Fast-forward to 2017 and one of the two most significant moments – the World Cup Final at Lord's. Compared with the tournament four years earlier, the final between England and India at the Home of Cricket showed the world what investment, exposure and attention could do for women's sport. There can be a few more important days.

Similarly, the T20 World Cup Final at Melbourne in 2020. Despite the continued (though diminishing) troll-spouted assertion that 'no one likes women's sport', 86,000 spectators attended a game watched by millions around the world. Days like that, when compared to India in 2013, show just how far the game has come in such a short space of time.

In terms of England, perhaps the most significant turning point was the professionalisation of the game around 2015 and the impact on players and coverage.

When England lost the Ashes at home that summer, there was – perhaps for the first time – media scrutiny and frustration at the on-field performance. I remember clearly a shell-shocked Charlotte Edwards being grilled after the Test match at Canterbury in a way that had not happened before. This felt like a defining moment that paid women's cricket the biggest compliment of all: 'If you're not performing, you're going to be held to account'. Nothing says a sport is being taken seriously like public frustration at poor results.

Finally, the advent of franchise leagues – led by the WBBL – has given so much opportunity for players to progress as professionals. The standards in the game over the past five years have grown remarkably.

Rather than Freddie Flintoff, Dale Steyn, Ricky Ponting or Virat Kohli, young girls can now see Heather Knight, Marizanne Kapp, Meg Lanning, Harmanpreet Kaur and so many more as role models they can try to emulate.

Insight: Jodie Hawkins, Sports Administrator

Women's cricket has come a long way in recent years. We've discussed a lot about the Australian women's cricket team, and I've had conversations with people in high performance who assume the Aussie women's team is more important than WBBL, which is true. But WBBL really opened the publicity door for women's cricket. If I was still there, I'd want to be playing finals at the SCG in front of packed houses. And another five years after that we should be playing at tier-one venues, the entire tournament, and tier-two venues shouldn't be part of our remit. So, that's where I'd like us to get to. I think countries like Australia, England and, to a point, India are going to have to lift their game a little bit as well. We have a responsibility as the powerhouses of international cricket to use our influence for good. That doesn't need to be beating people with a big stick. But it needs to be leading, helping develop this ICC Future Leaders program that I'm working with at the moment. This is about mentoring other women from some of the associate countries across the world to help them build their female cricket influence in their own countries. I think unless we all do it together, the old rising tide lifts all boats, that sort of stuff is really important. So, the bigger countries have a responsibility to use their influence and help support and drive the development of the women's game in other countries. I think we're starting to see some of that in India from the work that CA and the ECB have done. There is the women's IPL on the horizon; they should be investing more in the women's game; we're seeing more MOUs being developed between governing bodies and the female playing groups. But we absolutely have a responsibility to make sure that we hold other boards to account for that. And that's the influence we should be having while making sure we're investing in our own game as well. So, I have a bit of fear with women's cricket that we came out of the blocks really fast. We've built this great profile, and now all the other sports are chipping away and chipping away and chipping away. We need to keep investing to push forward. The women's game will never be as successful as the men's game unless we invest in it. It's important that we keep spending more than we're making around the women's game for the next probably 10 years. The men's game has a 150-year start from a PR point of view on the women's game. How do we accelerate that process? We have to be investing in it to keep accelerating. And we have to keep the benchmark high in our own country as well as for the other countries involved in cricket across the world to see that there is a benefit of engaging the other half of the population in your sport, both financially and from a goodwill piece.

Insight: Charlotte Edwards CBE, Coach and Former England Captain

The biggest difference now is that girls can have their first introduction to cricket at school and see that clear pathway to a club, their counties, a region and then on to playing for England. This is the thing that I'm most proud of when people ask me, as well as that a young girl can now have a career in cricket. This isn't just playing, it's umpiring, coaching and anything to do with the game.

For those 'older' women who were among those lost to the game as youngsters, we're now seeing opportunities for them to start playing through ECB softball festivals, or female hockey players who want a summer sport to play now have far greater opportunities and a generally more inclusive environment from clubs across the country.

For decades, girls' cricket suffered from a lack of coverage, opportunity and a culture of it being seen as 'not normal'. We're now seeing what can happen if all of these are addressed in a positive manner.

Insight: Henry Moeran, BBC Broadcaster and Producer

For any cultural activity to thrive and become popular, it has to be seen. Whether it's music, film or sport, there simply has to be a platform for people to enjoy it.

And audiences inevitably respond to what they're shown and how it's presented. If a women's cricket match is given the same treatment as a men's game, the audience will hopefully take it as seriously. If corners are cut or the commentators seem disinterested, then there is no incentive for the viewers/listeners to feel any passion for what they're following.

In the same way as having female experts on men's sport is crucial for the supporters to know it's a game for all, having male experts on women's sport is vital. No child is born to see any difference between men's and women's sport. The differences in perception are entirely manufactured.

Sport is sport and should be presented as such.

That may seem a simplistic mindset, and there is a long way to go. As every goalkeeping blunder in women's football is clipped, posted and ridiculed on social media, so is bad fielding in women's cricket. The old narrative that women's sport just isn't as good as – unfairly – meant that every mistake is magnified, while male blunders (which happen just as regularly) are laughed at briefly but without the vitriol.

The more women's sport is shown, analysed and critiqued by the experts and trusted voices that cover the men's game, the less, I hope, this will happen. Just as (happily) sports broadcasting is no longer the domain of only men, fully professional team sport isn't either.

Moments like Lord's in 2017 and the 2020 T20 World Cup Final should be just the start – but the investment and focus need to continue.

Young girls can now see a pathway in the game. They can play in school, then have the opportunity to join a club. If they're talented, their club could put them forward for county age group trials. From here, they can move up into the new regional structure and increasingly see the potential of a professional career in the sport. The most promising aspect of being a professional cricketer in England now is that you don't necessarily have to play for England to do this. You can sit below the England level and play at the regional level. Previously, the only fully professional players were those that reached the very top. This created a huge bottleneck of players who would have to make the choice of continuing playing or leaving the sport to find paid work elsewhere. This led to many players who may well have been good enough to play for England in the future having to quit. It also put a huge amount of pressure on those playing for England, knowing that the loss of their England contracts would mean the end of full-time training and a far more difficult path to force their way back into the international fold when the contracted girls could train full time and they couldn't.

Insight: Beth Barrett-Wild, Head of The Hundred Women's Competition & Female Engagement at England & Wales Cricket Board (ECB)

By showcasing the most talented female cricketers on the planet, on a big stage, alongside the men, we have an opportunity to continue to normalise cricket as a sport for women and girls, as much as it is for men and boys. I truly believe that The Hundred will be a gamechanger for women's sport.

In the men's game, if an England player lost their England contract they'd always have their county contract to fall back on as well as opportunities to play in the many franchise cricket leagues around the world. We're already seeing the benefit of these regional contracts, with players like Phoebe Graham in one of the current teams, as of this writing. Phoebe was working for Sky Sports but had the opportunity to move into a fully professional contract as a cricketer instead. This simply wouldn't have happened only a few years ago, and the game benefits greatly from having players as good as Phoebe being able to train full time. One would also hope that the introduction of the female equivalents of the Indian Premier League, Caribbean Premier League and many others won't be too far away for female players. Other players like Sophie Luff and Georgia Adams could also have been lost to the game had it not been for the regional structure and contracts – these are two high-quality players who at the time of writing had always been on the fringes of England. Imagine if we had lost two players of that quality because they had to commit to full-time jobs outside of cricket to earn a living. What a sad story that would be; luckily Georgia Adams is leading the Southern Vipers like an absolute boss and Sophie Luff continues to be a player at the top of coach's wish lists for all professional domestic competitions in England.

Insight: Charlotte Edwards CBE, Coach and Former England Captain

TV has really helped make the women's game more accessible; it has helped to show that the men's and women's formats are different, no better or worse, just different. Perceptions have changed and the vast majority are now fully accepting of women's and men's cricket.

We've also seen in the United Kingdom, the new *Hundred* competition where men's and women's cricket have been given equal billing. Young girls and boys could both go to the games and take inspiration from role models who look like them, which is so important. Tens of thousands of children are now growing up seeing cricket as not being suited to only one gender. These changes are starting to happen around the world as well. Australia has been leading the way with the Women's Big Bash, New Zealand is working towards this and we all hope that a women's IPL will happen soon as well.

The most beautiful thing about cricket today is that it's completely acceptable to have a girl play on a boys' team. It's just a part of cricket now. I see young boys coming down to watch women's cricket, they'll watch England, they'll watch the Vipers and it's lovely that so many young players are growing up seeing boys and girls as just cricketers, not defined by gender.

Insight: Charles Dagnall, Broadcaster

I think there have been many turning points in the women's game, but I will focus on three, most of these have happened in the last decade which shows the rapid rate of growth. Probably the most important turning point has been the exposure to the masses. I would argue prior to the women's World Cup in 2013, the odd tournament or series was covered, but since then the game has grown and that's because fans can see it. In turn, it has a knock-on effect when the game is shown on television then more people will go through the turnstiles. Until the matches were televised, the women's game was unfortunately marginalised. Via the same token, the mass use of social media has also been key to getting the game to more people, especially the younger generation. (I could go on here!)

The second is Franchise T20 cricket. Again, all televised, but there is a wider circle of quality players needed especially with the exposure. The addition of overseas players means a higher standard, and there's more access to high-quality coaching. It's helped in the BBL and in the United Kingdom with the KSL.

The last is the game going fully professional. Not too long ago it actually cost the players to play international cricket! With the advent of full contracts for England internationals and being paid for the franchises (probably not enough still), young players now have something to aspire to, and it's also a legitimate career path. They can dedicate all of their time to cricket, rather than doing it alongside a proper job. Much more needs to be done, but look at what has happened in Australia with 80 full-time players. Hopefully, that can be achieved around the world one day.

> There is a caveat. Two nations England and Australia are far more forward thinking than other nations.

To pick up on the point from Charles Dagnall around franchise cricket, perhaps one of the most recent and biggest indicators to date highlighting the commercial potential and popularity of women's cricket is the recently launched Fairbreak Invitational T20 Competition. Two points to note about this tournament are that it is privately funded so had to entice investors and sponsors, and the second is that it was ICC sanctioned which is a huge plus for a tournament of this kind. It was also televised around the world in the majority of countries that were represented in the tournament.

Insight: Ebony Rainford-Brent MBE, Broadcaster, Founder of ACE Programme and Former England Cricketer

I'd like to see the gap close between the top three women's cricket-playing nations and the rest of the world. This can be helped via much more knowledge sharing between nations. Having too big a gap between nations reduces competitiveness and affects the growth of the game.

Launched in May 2022, the first of its kind tournament saw six teams compete against each other over a period of two weeks. The teams were made up of international players from around the world including some of the world's biggest names such as Heather Knight, Deandra Dottin, Shabnim Ismail, Sophie Ecclestone, Sophie Devine and Suzie Bates to name a few. Perhaps the most welcoming aspect of the tournament is that the teams also included players from associate nations from all over the world – countries such as Rwanda, Brazil, Germany, Netherlands, Vanuatu, Nepal, Botswana and more had players featuring in the tournament. Players were paid as well as they ever had been in a franchise tournament for females, and the ultimate aim was to provide opportunity and genuine equality for players around the world.

Below is taken from the Fairbreak Website:

A World First Event

The Beginning of the Next Chapter in Women's Cricket

*The FairBreak Invitational 2022 (The Tournament) is an ICC sanctioned competition that will take place on **1–15 May 2022** in Dubai in conjunction with Cricket Hong Kong. This six-team tournament is made up of players from all around the world and will be the world's first privately funded tournament in women's cricket history with the leading healthcare group Gencor as the lead sponsor.*

WHY SHOULD WE GROW GIRLS' CRICKET?

The first answer to this question should probably be 'why on earth wouldn't we!'

Clubs

The benefits of starting and developing girls' programmes for clubs are enormous. Every cricket club across the world faces pressures around membership, finances, attracting volunteers, coaches, community engagement, on-field success, sponsorship and the overall development of the sport. With the boys' game so well developed and mature, the possibilities to grow are more limited. The opportunities very clearly lie within girls' cricket. With the women's game now moving very rapidly into the mainstream, clubs would be missing out on so many positive things if they don't put a significant emphasis on girls' cricket very quickly.

Clubs have a very real chance to double their membership in a very short space of time. With more members comes more chance of volunteers and new coaches from the families and friends of those new members. It isn't difficult to then see the added revenue potential from both membership fees and behind the club bar!

Girls' cricket can also provide clubs with opportunities to develop more and better links with schools in their areas. Imagine the possibilities for a club to develop links to all-girls school in the 1990s. Let's just say they were relatively limited in comparison to what they are now. The same goes for mixed-gender schools, why would a club ignore 50% of the kids in a school as potential new members? If clubs reach full capacity with regard to their facilities, can deeper partnerships with schools provide added potential to offset this or look towards sharing facilities?

Attracting sponsorship is something that a thriving girls' team can really help to drive as well. Plenty of local companies and brands would love to be associated with girls' sports and may be far more willing to sponsor a girls' team than a boys' team if their product or service is more oriented towards females. With the England team, the first time we ever saw dual sponsorship was with Vodafone. They initially only sponsored the men's team before moving to be involved with both. A few years down the line we saw Kia become the first brand that said they only wanted to sponsor the women's team. Businesses now often have a much more targeted focus on women, and women's sports are an excellent opportunity for them to get their message out there. There's also a far greater emphasis on companies wanting to display their corporate social responsibility. Getting involved with promoting female sports that have suffered so much under-representation for such a long time is a great way for them to do this.

Many clubs are now seeing separate sponsors for their women's and men's teams. All of a sudden clubs' sponsorship possibilities can double.

Insight: Charlotte Edwards CBE, Coach and Former England Captain

For a school or a club, it's now a no-brainer that you have to give a girl the same opportunities as a boy. Every school in this country should now have a girls' cricket programme. It's our national summer sport and this should be reflected. For clubs, a girl's programme brings so much. Clubs should be as welcoming and diverse as possible. Cricket is for everyone – male, female, disabled and able-bodied. Talking to clubs now, there's been a big shift in attitudes, bar takings and grant potential are also significantly increased. It's the biggest growth area of the game, so why wouldn't you get involved?

Players

I hope we can all agree that sport in general has immeasurable benefits to girls (and of course boys), no matter which one they're involved with. It'd take an entirely separate book to discuss areas like health, fitness, confidence, respect for others, life skills, social aspects, winning and losing gracefully, leadership, discipline and so many others besides. Cricket undoubtedly provides all of these, but also some that I think are relatively unique to our sport.

With many sports, there's the possibility that a young girl is either good at it or not. Taking football as an example, they may very well experience what they perceive as 'failure' very quickly, which can put them off returning to it. With cricket, you've got four different elements in one for them to try and see if it's something suited to them. It's a lovely thing for a school or a club to have beginner players try batting, bowling, fielding and wicketkeeping, giving them far more opportunities to find something they either enjoy or show a talent for (or both).

Insight: Fran Wilson – Professional Cricketer and former England Player

If you're keen to improve your fielding, it's a great idea to play lots of different sports when you're young. I always felt like the reason I could dive around the cricket field was due to playing a lot of rugby as a youngster.

Insight: Heather Knight OBE, England Captain

Playing boys' cricket definitely helped my development. I played pretty much all-boys cricket until I was 13, just because it was a higher standard. I was lucky to have a lot of one-to-one coaching at my club where they were just very specific to me and helped me develop quite quickly. I trusted the coaches which was a great feeling. My cricket club Plymstock was super welcoming; they made me feel like I wasn't different at all, which I obviously was being the only girl. They made sure I was looked after in terms of changing rooms if there were female changing rooms or making sure I was aware of where the female toilets were, which is where I used to change pretty much all the time.

On top of this, we often see the less sporty young girls having the chance to excel and enjoy the other elements of cricket; the tactics, the communication skills or simply the spirit of cricket. The feeling of being part of a team and community should never be underestimated as one of the best benefits of sport and indeed cricket can bring to a young person's life.

The friendship aspect of cricket is also incredibly significant. Sports like hockey or football are relatively short games, where the players turn up, play the game and then it's done. With cricket, you're with a group of people for a longer period of time. The friendships fostered through cricket are built on much more than just turning up and playing. The players are in that really special cricket club environment where they can spend many years. If you're on the batting side and not actually batting, there are often seven or eight players sat on the boundary just chatting and laughing. They may not know it at the time, but they're developing social skills and friendships that will last them a lifetime.

There's also the element of individuality within the team that cricket provides. Not all young girls would naturally gravitate to a team sport, so cricket can provide that as well.

It's a sport with a wide variety of possibilities for young girls to find the right element for them and hopefully a long-term love of the game.

Insight: Henry Moeran, BBC Broadcaster and Producer

Though a somewhat sad way to look at the advancement of skill, perhaps the easiest measure is 'Well what are the criticisms?'

For a long time, fielding had been the area that detractors of the game would pick out as inferior. In recent years, however, the women's game has seen the standard of fielding shoot forward. Those jarring moments with the ball creeping over the boundary edge have been largely replaced by the sort of viral moments that can do wonders for a sport's exposure and growth.

So much of sport is now consumed in bite-sized social media chunks, and a flying catch or boundary save could be that moment that makes a young person – previously uninterested in cricket – sit up and take notice.

It is no coincidence that investment, professionalism and full-time coaching lead to female athletes showing that they can be every bit as good as their male counterparts.

The other regular criticism was the 'power' in the women's game.

The fact that England women hit more ODI sixes in 2016–2017 than they did in 1973–2015 tells its own story.

Once again, thanks to full-time professionalism and coaching, the women's game has proved these criticisms to be unfair.

The women's game was unrecognisable some 20 years ago. The opportunities, the training, the coaching, the TV coverage, the attitudes, the culture, the support from sponsors and the number of girls taking part have all increased dramatically.

This is also a nice time to acknowledge the many amazing people who did so much prior to the 20 years ago we are often referencing in this book. There are too many names to mention, so many females throughout the decades have had so much impact in getting the game to where it is now that it is often easy to forget them. These players, administrators, coaches and general supporters of the women's game will rarely get the recognition they deserve; women's cricket just wasn't televised, written about or even spoken about in the public domain as it is now, so it is a shame that many of these people will go unnoticed. However, it is the job of those of us involved in the game and in books like this to ensure we are always acknowledging and tipping our hat to those who trod the path to make it a heck of a lot easier for those playing today.

Insight: Charles Dagnall, Broadcaster

All skills have improved in the white ball games over the past decade. All the tricks that bowlers possess (numerous types of slower balls, bouncers, etc.) have gotten better; batters all now play innovative shots 360 degrees off the field, plus they hit with way more power and the fielding (bar Lydia!) is on a different level. The other aspect is tactically with more series played and more high-profile global competitions, captains are more astute.

The good news is that the potential for further growth is enormous. We're just at the beginning of what could and should be a very special time for female cricket in the long term. I hope this book can make some contribution to more young girls and adult females playing and loving the sport as I did, and still do.

Insight: Adam Collins, Broadcaster and Journalist

Domestic investment has been a huge part of the story. The WBBL and Kia Super League have created a sense of momentum around what's possible for the women's game. These arrived a little before the 2017 World Cup where there was greater ambition for broadcasters to cover the games as well. This brought more eyeballs to women's cricket in a way that just wasn't possible before.

By the end of the first WBBL tournament, there were relatively modest expectations as to the potential viewership. These expectations were exceeded many times over to the point where they had to shuffle later games over to the main channels to meet the needs of the viewers. This was a huge signal that 'if you build it they will come'.

This in turn shifted the attitude of cricket administrators around the world, including those who were previously cynical who saw the opportunity for revenue generation.

This saw a memorandum of understanding with the Australian women's team in 2017 and the rapid increase in salaries.

We've seen this translate across the world of cricket with professional female players appearing in so many more cricket-playing nations. We've seen players like Mithali Raj building huge social media platforms where they can and do make the game so much more visible.

We're living in a generation where female players don't see the same barriers as was the case for so long.

Insight: Alison Mitchell, Broadcaster

There have been several key moments in the development of women's professional cricket in the United Kingdom. An important year was 2005; England's women won the Ashes in the same summer that England's men won the most extraordinary Ashes series ever played. A joint victory celebration in Trafalgar Square then put the women on stage – quite literally – alongside the men, in a way that hadn't been done before. That was one moment of publicity in time. However, the advent of Chance to Shine coaching contracts soon after that helped England women players to juggle playing for their country with flexible employment – a significant enabler and an early step towards professionalism. Chance to Shine in itself began to take cricket into state schools, using women players alongside men as coaches and ambassadors and starting to normalise cricket as a sport for girls as well as boys, among children of primary school age.

England's double World Cup wins in 2009 played a bigger role in providing the impetus to press for further investment from the ECB, as well as putting the game on the map in terms of the mainstream media in the United Kingdom. At the 50-over World Cup in Australia earlier in the year, I had been the only travelling UK journalist covering the England team. When England played Australia in a semi-final double header with the men's semi at the Oval in June, a scintillating 76 not out by Claire Taylor captivated seasoned cricket writers and commentators who were present because of the men's match to come. Some members of the media had barely taken the women's game seriously before. Now they were sitting up, taking notice and liking what they were seeing.

The 50-over World Cup earlier that year had been the first to be played under the auspices of the ICC, which had taken over the running of the women's game in 2005. At a global level, the ICC's investment in women's cricket has been crucial, in particular increasing the visibility of World Cup events through live streaming and social media, whereupon an audience could be demonstrated and thus later moving towards televising all World Cup matches. This wouldn't have happened though without countries like England and Australia leading the way in developing their professionalism in the decade from 2010 to 2020; from tour fees and retainer contracts, to full professional deals with maternity clauses now. They have developed a domestic professional and semi-professional base and established the Women's Big Bash League in Australia, and the Kia Super League in the United Kingdom, which has now been replaced by The Hundred. These leagues are well supported by television, which has been a vital medium in normalising the sport for women through visibility. In the United Kingdom, England's victory in the 2017 World Cup Final at a sold-out Lord's was a game-changing moment in demonstrating the appeal of the women's game and its ability to captivate young and family-friendly audiences, different to the traditional followers of the men's game. Commentating on the winning moment for BBC Test Match Special and hosting the trophy presentation for a global audience of millions remain a highlight of my career for its significance in the landscape of the women's game in the United Kingdom, as much as for the excitement of the moment itself. Three years on, that final was usurped by a record crowd of more than 86,174 at the MCG for an exceedingly well-marketed Women's T20 World Cup Final, won by Australia but inspiring to all.

Throughout this time, the number of women commentators in the media has grown significantly, to the point that opportunities are now plentiful for current and former players. Women's voices are actively sought after on both radio and television, which is a far cry from the years I spent as the only female commentary voice in the English game. The rise of the women's game itself and the increased profile of the players have helped with this. And hearing knowledgeable women describe and debate cricket – men's or women's – sends a strong message that the game is for all.

Cricket in England and Wales has never been in a better place in terms of the opportunities available for women as a career path. The capacity for growth is still enormous, and that's the most exciting thing.

CHAPTER SUMMARY

- Women and girls cricket is growing quickly, but we're not even close to realising the full potential

- Young girls can now see a full pathway to a professional career in the game

- Recreational and club cricket have an enormously significant role to play

- The benefits to all clubs and schools to grow their female cricket programmes are huge

CHAPTER 2

How to Develop a Successful Club or School Programme

There's no doubt that female cricket is experiencing a rapid participation rise in both schools and clubs, but we also know that not every club or school has a full programme. The good news is that there's a clear willingness from the vast majority to do just this. Knowing where to start and how to progress is often the hardest part. This chapter is all about just this.

STARTING A CLUB PROGRAMME

Like anything, building from the bottom up is vital. Sometimes it seems the more straightforward option is to go for the quick wins, especially if you already have a group of late teens and senior women ready and waiting to form a team.

It is easy to focus all your efforts on developing this particular group which on many occasions will see success in a short period of time, but in the long-term can lack sustainability – especially when you factor in teenage dropouts and players retiring at certain ages.

The most successful female clubs have a sharp focus on the youngest groups ensuring there is provision to offer a consistent and recurring training programme delivered by reliable, enthusiastic and knowledgeable coaches. This is not to say *don't* focus on the ready and waiting group of female adults who are keen and ready to go. Absolutely make sure they are provided with the training, games, people and facilities that they need but don't make it your *only* focus, simply because they are most likely to bring you tangible results. Long-term sustainability is by far the most important element to consider.

Working from the bottom up means a lot of hard work from dedicated and passionate individuals. Let's start with a practical shopping list of ideas to start you off in the right direction. It is so important to make the club environment a welcoming one and factoring in these will help you achieve this:

1. **Who will be there week in and week out?** You need to identify at least two committed, enthusiastic and knowledgeable coaches to ensure the players have a familiar face each week. This is often the first hurdle clubs struggle to get past with coaches coming and going and changing all too regularly. Consistency in the coaches is vital in keeping the players engaged, forming relationships and building lasting success. It does help to have a female involved in the coaching setup for a number of reasons, but it is also worth pointing out that there are lots of fantastic male coaches who are super impactful in this space as well.

2. **Facilities and equipment:** It's really important to ensure the girls and women feel entirely equal and included at the club. With this in mind, make sure they use the best facilities you have to offer. This includes everything from changing rooms, nets, pitch access and equipment. This isn't a suggestion to say that women and girls should have any priority over boys' and men's cricket, but rather to have use of everything equally – there is no reason why this shouldn't happen. It is also important to make sure your female toilets have sanitary bins as well as extra tampons/sanitary towels on hand within the toilets.

   With regard to equipment, you'll learn more in the kit and equipment chapter, but for some extra emphasis, there are increasingly more brands creating female-specific ranges featuring more fitted equipment. It's a really important distinction between the male and female games and another step towards helping your female players feel fully part of the game. Take a look at The Female Cricket Store to see what might be suitable for your players (www.thefemalecricketstore.com).

3. **Female representation on club committee:** According to Clare Connor (Managing Director of Women's Cricket at the ECB) this 'changes the culture in cricket clubs to make them more inclusive for women and girls'. Many cricket clubs have fantastic, open-minded and forward-thinking committees who go above and beyond to support their women's and girls' section; however, this isn't always the case. That is why it is so important to make sure that every part of your club is represented and has a voice on the committee, including the women's and girls' section. We've all seen too many examples of poorly representative committees across many sports discussing issues for people who they have little understanding of. Let's make cricket fully represented across all aspects of the game.

4. **Build links with local schools:** This can't be over-emphasised in terms of having consistent groups of new players. Cricket clubs that engage with their local schools will have more chances of building and more importantly *sustaining* thriving women's and girls' section of the club. There are a number of ways you can build links with schools, which include sharing facilities and coaching personnel. The most important first step though is to go and speak to your local schools and discuss how you can build mutually beneficial links. The possibilities are endless.

5. **Music:** If you can, have music playing at the session; as simple as it sounds, it's amazing to see the effect this has on the players' enjoyment levels. Having music is also a great ice-breaker during training as it helps relax the less outgoing or less confident players. I'd also suggest allowing the players to take turns in creating the playlists for each session – in a small way this can also help with

player retention, knowing they can pick their own playlist the following week means they will definitely attend.

6. **Someone to run the BBQ:** Cricket clubs have a reputation for being social places and emphasising this is a very underrated way of attracting and retaining players. Having the bar open with a BBQ running (weather permitting of course!) at training sessions and during games is also a great way to engage with the parents. A Friday evening training session or match provides a lovely start to the weekend, giving them a relaxing and social environment where they can have a couple of drinks while their children are playing sport. Please do be mindful of those who don't drink alcohol or eat meat in both your advertising or events and you'll start seeing the benefits of a fully inclusive, fun and vibrant setting.

7. **Do it for the right reason:** Lastly but arguably the most important point. People within the game are well-aware that governing bodies have the ability to fund clubs for things such as new facilities, extra coaches or new equipment, and this funding often comes off the back of clubs meeting certain criteria – as you would expect. Often, part of the criteria to access this funding is that they have a cricket offering for women and girls; this of course is again how it should be but on a small number of occasions, some clubs opt to set up women and girls offering in a slapdash manner just to meet the criteria without any real interest in making the offering genuine. When this happens, it's not going to benefit anyone. So, if you are going to set up a women's and girls' section of your club, make sure you throw all the bells and whistles at it and there will be no doubt it will be a roaring success.

RETAINING PLAYERS AT YOUR CLUB

One of the most asked questions by clubs running girls' sections is how do we stop girls from dropping out in their teenage years? The honest answer is that you can't entirely, but you can do things which ensure that, even if they do drop out, the club can still continue to be successful. The first is the point we have already covered, focus on getting as many girls involved at a young age. This is then simply a numbers game: the more you have, the better chance you have of being sustainable even when the inevitable dropouts happen.

The second thing you can do is to create an environment and offering that caters for both the serious and social cricketers. We will never be able to stop every player from dropping out, but we do have to factor in the reason why they might be dropping out. See below some examples:

- Focus on other sports
- Develop other interests
- Lose interest in cricket
- Too competitive
- Not competitive enough
- Don't like hardball cricket

Some of these will always be out of our control but others are not. The competitive element is a really interesting one. From the point of view that it can become too competitive, it's important for the people delivering the cricket to identify players' reasons for playing to allow them to cater for what they need. As coaches, it can be really easy to focus on results, outcomes and techniques while forgetting the reason most people play sports. It is no coincidence that the shopping list outlined earlier doesn't really focus on the performance side of things. The social element for young players is something we must never forget, and it is important that those girls are identified and catered for while still being able to provide the 'serious' players with the competitive environment that they thrive in. This is also why it is important to have at least two coaches at every session to make sure the 'competitive' and 'social' players are enjoying the right environment.

There will be large number of girls who are competitive; they are focussed on the results, and they do want to develop better techniques and have ambitions to play professional cricket. This is where ensuring these players are identified and play in the same group is so important. Another approach to this, especially if you are yet to have the numbers you need for this type of training group, is to offer the girls the opportunity to play with the boys – this will be covered more broadly in another chapter but generally it is a great way to challenge girls who want to progress, and it keeps them engaged in a more challenging environment.

THE PROGRESSION OF GIRLS' CRICKET IN SCHOOLS – THEN AND NOW

The girls' cricketing landscape in schools has changed hugely over the last 20 years. From having a limited to often non-existent offering in many schools, cricket has now become a prominent and, in a lot of cases, the main summer sport in both state and private schools.

Experience from current 'older' players suggests being a girl playing cricket in a school 20+ years ago meant you had to be of a certain ability, as your only option would have been to play with the boys. So, if you were going to take the place of one of your male schoolmates, you would have had to have proven yourself more so than your peers just to get an opportunity.

It would be a safe bet to say girls' cricket in schools was very much 'not the done thing' with the main focus being on rounders during the summer term. People will be familiar with the sight during a PE or games lesson if they were to drive past a school on a summer's day. One half of the field (if the school was lucky to have one!) was set up with boys playing 'kwik' cricket, or even hardball games depending on the age. On the other side of the field, there would have been a lovely game of rounders taking place by the girls. It is important to point out early that rounders in terms of the sport itself is fantastic; it was a sport many girls have loved to play at school and in PE lessons, and it certainly has its place, but it is also important to highlight a few points which emphasise why cricket will benefit girls more than rounders in the long run (I'm biased, but I think for good reason!). Both sports offer many positives to the sporting community, but the below highlights why cricket in the summer should take the front seat at schools for girls, not just boys. So for people yet to be convinced, hopefully, this will help.

1. **Pathway:** This is the biggest plus cricket brings to schools when it comes to keeping girls engaged with sport. Yes, cricket can be played at school, but being able to direct girls to their local cricket club is massive. We're all aware of the dropout rates we see at 15+ and having a club to play with post-schooling is a huge positive.

    The step to a club doesn't stop there; there is a full pathway provided from the youngest age groups all the way up to 70+, giving players a lifetime of involvement in a game.

2. **Inclusive:** If delivered in the right way, cricket can be a hugely inclusive game. A PE lesson for cricket can be made up of different skill circuits with the girls working in small groups during regular rotations. This type of lesson keeps everyone active and engaged which is often one of the perceived downfalls in cricket. This is also the case when it comes to match play; there are many different formats and adaptations which can be used to ensure the games are fun, engaging and encouraging everyone to get involved.

3. **Role models:** The well-known phrase 'You can't be what you can't see' applies to females playing sport and trying to encourage others to take it up. A women's Ashes series took place in Australia in 2003 with the first Test Match being played at The Gabba, Brisbane, Australia. Cricket fans will be familiar with the multicoloured seating, one of the main features at the stadium. For a men's Ashes Test Match not one of those seats would be visible because of the people sitting in them, but in 2003, as one of the world's best female fast bowlers, Cathryn Fitzpatrick was ripping through the England batting lineup in what was one of the finest bowling displays the women's game would have seen, every single one of those seats was vacant.

The event was like a piece of tumbleweed in the world of sport, while in a parallel universe there would have been young girls with a passion for the game and no doubt stacks of ability who just wouldn't have known what was possible. It makes you wonder how many girls stopped playing cricket just because they couldn't see what was possible.

Nowadays, if you turn on the television, tune in to your radio, scroll through social media or pick up the latest weekend newspapers, the chances are there will be females playing cricket and the sporting nation will know about it. Young girls can see their idols in action and can see a tangible pathway to aspire towards.

For teachers, they can go above and beyond directing them to their local cricket club, they can take them on a school trip to see their heroes in action and even better; they can tell their pupils that making a living out of playing cricket is now possible – something many people would have not thought possible many years ago.

4. **Media:** The coverage the game receives and the accessibility to role models perhaps go hand in hand. In 2005, the women's 50-over World Cup in South Africa took place in front of precisely no one other than friends and families of players participating in the tournament.

This changed.

As we spoke about in the opening chapter, perhaps a watershed moment in the women's game happened in 2020 when the Melbourne Cricket Ground was filled with over 80,000 people turning up to watch the women's World T20 Final between Australia and India. It is the increased coverage in the media that also makes cricket more accessible for females of all ages. This very much applies to older female adults as well as younger females and is a brilliant reason to develop your programme.

5. **Character building**: The phrase linked to cricket and something those involved with the sport I would like to put the spotlight on is the 'spirit of cricket'.

Cricket is a game that owes much of its unique appeal to the fact that it should be played not only within its Laws but also within the Spirit of the Game. Any action which is seen to abuse this spirit causes injury to the game itself. The major responsibility for ensuring the spirit of fair play rests with the captains.

In a world where sporting integrity is increasingly emphasised, the game of cricket offers a way to influence and develop young people's characters – boys and girls. From winning and losing gracefully to accepting defeat with a smile on your face, or at least with a firm handshake and looking into your opponent's eye to say well done, cricket is unique in the teachings it can offer youngsters in later life.

Schools aren't always, nor should they be trying to produce the next Heather Knights, Smriti Mandhana, Ellyse Perry or Deandra Dottin but more often than not they will be striving to ensure their pupils leave as decent human beings. Cricket is a fantastic vehicle to teach such important life lessons.

WHERE ARE WE NOW WITH GIRLS' CRICKET IN SCHOOLS?

Already highlighted is the big change on the PE curriculum at GCSE level in England, in which rounders was taken off and replaced by cricket in 2015 as the main striking and fielding sport in the summer. For cricket fans, this was a hugely welcome change but for many, especially PE teachers who had no experience of cricket and love for rounders, it was received coldly. Understandably so, if you ask anyone who has never played or watched cricket before what they think of the game you'll often hear:

- It's long, complicated and boring
- Doesn't it go on for days?
- It's too technical

- There are only two people ever involved
- The clothing is awful!

A favourite question from cricket novices is 'who's winning?' Often asked halfway through a game – which when you think about it actually isn't a silly question at all. Sports like football, hockey and netball allow you to give clear definitive answers at any time in the game but cricket certainly does not. You can understand why people, teachers especially, have had such an apprehension when it comes to understanding the game, let alone having to go and deliver it.

However, this apprehension has been short-lived. When teachers are shown a fun and broken-down way to deliver the game which takes away all the barriers previously experienced (see www.cricketforgirls.com for more info on this), we are seeing a huge shift in the excitement around the game of cricket in schools. Long gone are the days when the first thing a child learns is the forward defence. Young children want to experience the most fun parts of sport, and it is important to remember that when we are introducing and developing a girls' cricket programme. First impressions are important in all walks of life, and sport is no different – the first experience of a new sport for any young person is the most important one.

Before moving on to the next part of this chapter, it is important to acknowledge the many challenges schools and teachers can sometimes face when delivering girls' cricket:

- Lack of expertise and knowledge
- Facilities
- Equipment
- How does it differ from boys' cricket?
- What format to play when?
- How soon should we move to hardball cricket?
- Existing negative perceptions of cricket from teachers, pupils and parents

The next section of this chapter will go on to provide advice and tips on how to deliver girls' cricket in schools.

CRICKET IN SCHOOLS: HOW TO SET UP AND DELIVER AN EFFECTIVE GIRLS' CRICKET PROGRAMME

There are some vital ingredients to running and delivering a successful girl programme:

1. **Make the first impression the best one** – This is key when delivering cricket to a group of girls for the first time. There are key questions you need to answer when planning your programme from when the pupils arrive in the school to when they progress to the oldest age. Are the players completely new to the game? If so, stay away from the technique and put the spotlight on fun and success. Have they already been exposed to hardball cricket? If so, you will have to ensure there is a hardball offering for that group of girls straight away.

   We can't hide from the fact that cricket can be and is a very technical game, but there are ways in which the game can be completely stripped back and presented in much simpler forms. For example, batting can be delivered in a very technical way, but it can also be delivered in the most fun way which is simply by giving players multiple opportunities to hit the ball as hard and as far as they can. There is little to no technique involved in setting this up.

2. **Facilities** – This is no different to what we have suggested for clubs. If you are a mixed school that plays both boys' and girls' cricket, then please do not palm your girls off with second-grade facilities while the boys use the best facilities week in and week out. There is no reason why these facilities cannot be shared and

sharing this doesn't mean the girls get to use the 'first XI square' once a year. To quote the brilliant Billie Jean King:

'Everyone thinks women should be thrilled when we get crumbs, and I want women to have cake, the icing and the cherry on top too'.

In this instance, sharing the cake equally will suffice.

3. **Language Used – Internal and External Coaching Cues –** Internal coaching cues are often used when players know what needs correcting and there is a certain element of existing knowledge of technique involved in the game. They tend to be used for more experienced players.

An example of these in action using the front-foot drive off a batting T as the skill being coached:

Internal cues for introducing the front-foot drive

Lean into the ball

Have a higher backswing

Have a strong top hand

Show the full face of the bat

Bend your front knee

Have your head over the ball

Finish with a high elbow (what does that even mean?)

External cues for introducing the front-foot drive

Using this example, you can have either a target using two cones or a wall.

'Hit the ball as hard as you can through the target from this starting position' – physical demonstration from the coach.

Straight away you can see the difference between these two types of coaching cues. External cues take away any thought about technique and focus on the outcome rather than what the movement should look like and feel like to achieve the outcome.

External cues are much more effective for beginners new to the game, while internal coaching cues are prescriptive and can also be ambiguous. More often than not players will problem-solve and find ways to achieve the outcome – the beauty of using external cues for beginners often means players will tick off a lot of the techniques naturally. And if they don't, once you have given them the simple external cue of 'hit the ball through that target as hard as you can', you will then be able to walk around and spot any common technical themes where participants may benefit from more technical feedback or internal cues.

4. **Formats: What format to play and when?** – There is an argument to suggest that the format a girl, school or year group play should be dependent on experience *not* age. Unlike boys' cricket in school (as a general assumption although it is acknowledged that this can also vary – especially between independent and state schools) where there is an established and expected path to follow when it comes to cricket formats at certain ages, this is not the case for girls. The reason for this is that the development of girls' cricket is at varying points depending on which school or area they are in. For example, there may be primary and prep schools that offer and deliver a substantial girls' cricket programme from year 3 upwards. This means when girls move on to secondary school they are doing so with three- to four-year experiences of playing cricket. Compare that to schools that may only offer cricket to their year 6 students, or quite possibly nothing at all – they are then going to secondary school with no experience of the game at all.

The varied stages schools are at can cause some challenges, in particular when it comes to fixtures. There have been many occasions when a school in one area has been delivering hardball cricket and playing T20 games. In this situation, there has to be a compromise. Yes, the more advanced schools will want better competition, but they must also understand that by compromising and perhaps playing pairs cricket over T20 cricket, they are helping with the development of schools nearby who, by having the experience of playing pairs, will then develop to be able to eventually play T20 therefore benefiting the more advanced schools. It could be argued that there is no benefit in the more advanced school not being willing to flex when it comes to playing a less challenging format like pairs. This point can also be applied the other way around, if a school is keen to move onto T20 but are yet to have any match play then the school already playing T20 can help bring the other school up to speed.

The image below shows suggestions of what formats to play when, and it is important to note that these suggestions are based on experience rather than age.

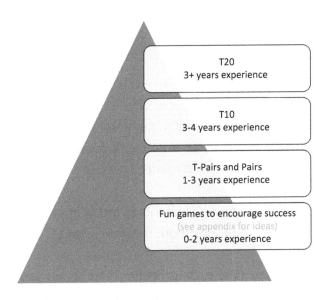

It's important to note that this model should be used with flexibility. There may be occasions when players are ready to progress more quickly while there may be other occasions when players are happily playing pairs cricket. It is also important to highlight that all of these formats should be offered with a softball option to ensure all players are catered for whatever their ambition and motivation.

T-Pairs: T-Pairs is very similar to pairs cricket, but it caters for the fact that while youngsters are learning the game it is likely the bowling will be slightly wayward. The consequence of this is that the batter will not have much opportunity to be able to hit the ball if they are facing wide after wide. T-Pairs cricket uses batting Tee's on either side of the crease lines and if the ball is bowled outside of the Batting Tees, then a wide is given along with a free hit to the batter. There will be a batting tee on each side of the batting crease with a ball on top and this is where the batter will take their free hit from.

WHEN TO INTRODUCE HARDBALL CRICKET?

This is another common question asked by teachers and coaches, and the answer isn't a concrete one. It is often driven by the players, and year groups may vary in how quickly they are ready or want to progress. Using the formats model as an example, it could be suggested that hardball cricket can start to be introduced between one and three years of experience.

Below are some important elements to factor in when introducing hardball, and we will go into more detail in Chapter 5 about all of these.

Start with isolated skills such as fielding. This allows you to control the environment such as starting with close catching in pairs, picking up a moving ball or overarm throwing at a target. This allows the players to get used to the feel of the ball.

Avoid going straight into a net or game situation – this is an environment where conditions cannot be controlled, for example, erratic bowlers or fielders exposed to the ball being hit too hard at them.

Equipment – before going into the nets, allow the players to get used to the equipment and how it should be worn; relay races can be a good way to help with this.

Break down the skills – for bowlers, let them bowl at a target without a batter to start with; they will need to get used to the change in weight of a cricket ball which can affect their release point. Similarly with batting; allow them to practice a range of shots in the nets with underarm feeds rather than against a bowler; the bats will be heavier compared to the plastic ones and the harder ball will also be a change for them.

By ticking the above items off the list will mean that players will start their hardball journey with more confidence and willingness to continue and most importantly enjoy the game.

Hayes School Case Study: *Hayes School is a state school based in Kent. They have been delivering girls' cricket for over 20 years and have done so with success and without access to extravagant facilities. This case study is helpful for any school in a similar position but also for schools that need advice on how best to deliver a thriving girls' cricket programme for all ages and abilities.*

Hayes School in Kent has been delivering a successful girls' cricket programme for a number of years. If you were to drive past the school a lunchtime or after school during the summer, you would see the school field filled with both boys and girls playing cricket, sometimes mixed but usually separate. On hearing this you might assume there is an immaculately kept cricket square, with multiple cut wickets, a scoreboard and a pavilion, but there isn't. They have one artificial wicket in the middle of the field. What they don't have in facilities they make up in expertise, opportunity and the value placed on girls' cricket by their staff. This is a brilliant example of emphasising the importance of having the passion and willingness to make something work even when there might be perceived barriers. Here are some insights from the Head of PE – Joe Healy.

How You Have Engaged with Pupils to Take up the Sport?

All girls in KS3 and 4 are involved in cricket within PE lessons throughout the year but more often during the summer term. This feeds into an extra-curricular option which is based on two levels. One allows for mini games using wind balls and plastic bats where the girls enjoy small-sided games throughout the session with a small amount of technical input from our staff, and a second option is a progressive session with a hardball in preparation for competitive cricket. In addition, those girls with the required confidence also take part in boys' cricket training and play for the boys' teams.

What Are the Focus Areas in Your Programmes? Skills, Games or Fun?

Our focus is opportunity and excellence. All girls can play cricket, and sessions are tailored to suit the needs of those involved. No girl is turned away, and all sessions offer fun and challenge. We also have girls-only fixtures against other girls, and our girls' team play in local and county boys-only competitions to ensure that they remain motivated throughout the summer should we struggle to play enough games.

How/When Do You Progress to Hardball?

This depends on the students. If a core of young girls comes to us with that experience, then we introduce them immediately to hardball and make them play with the boys, but we recognise that this is not always appropriate, and many of our girls play cricket with wind balls. This is especially evident in curriculum lessons.

How Have You Engaged with the Local Community such as Local Cricket Clubs to Form Partnerships?

We are blessed to be across the road from a club that values girls' cricket so much that it made sense to engage with them. This includes sharing facilities, expertise and giving our girls exit routes into a club. Many of our girls are able to taste cricket at the club for free because of our partnership, and the PE teachers will take a new group of years 7's every year to the club's first summer session so that they feel a little more at ease when going to a new club for the first time.

What Was Important in Terms of Keeping the Pupils Engaged?

Regularity of training and games is key. We tried to ensure that we had at least two PE teachers at each session so that sessions are very rarely cancelled. Experience tells me that some students lose interest when sessions and games are being cancelled all of the time. We also enter the girls into boys' competitions and play against established cricketing school's D teams which ensure a competitive game of cricket for our younger girls.

How Do You Keep Pupils Interested When They Enter Their Teenage Years, Which Is a Key Group in Terms of Possible Dropouts?

Obviously, this has its challenges, but I believe this starts in year 7. Our girls know of cricket from day one. We do not play competitive rounders anymore. Cricket is the main summer sport and when the girls are playing in PE lessons and having fun, it is much easier to engage them in games for the school.

How Have You Built from the Bottom Up to Ensure You Have a Steady Flow of Players Coming Through?

This includes opening our indoor nets for the local club to use on a weekend, encouraging girls to play with the boys from year 7 onwards and incorporating cricket throughout the school. We also have role models who we celebrate all of the time.

Richmond CC Case Study, Richie Stubbs Richmond CC has been able to build a successful girls' section and here I have highlighted a few key ingredients for creating and running a girls' section in any cricket club.

What Do You Think Are the Most Immediate Priorities for a Club to Set up a New Program?

The most important things you'll need are a supportive chairperson and management boards and a concentration on attracting volunteers.

With the growth in popularity of the sport, you might end up with more, but smaller team sizes, like football, hockey and rugby are doing. But the knock-on effect is that you'll need more parents to help because you might only have 6 children not 11, and you still need two umpires, a scorer and the pitches. Volunteers are crucial as the game grows.

How Do You Work with Other Clubs in the Same Area?

We have a strong emphasis on sharing best practices with all our fellow clubs. In many ways, it is a joint journey. The more players each team attracts, the more chances of relatively even competition, which is ultimately what players enjoy most. It's not about winning or losing, you just don't want to smash people or get smashed, so anything in the middle is good. Working with other clubs can only help this and so it benefits all of us.

How Do You Help Players Move through the Pathways and Age Groups?

The pathway or the transition from junior cricket to adult cricket is really important to emphasise. Girls can actually do it much earlier than boys so they can see a clear vision throughout their time playing. Once you get to a good playing standard, there's less disparity in the strength and speed of the bowlers who are slightly older. We often find that on the female circuit the county under 15 bowlers actually end up being the bowler for older women's teams. It's really important you think of it as a joined-up thing and get this message across to the players.

Skipton CC Case Study: David Bunyan *Skipton CC have set up a hugely successful new programme in a relatively quick time and explain exactly how they've done it. David is also the lead coach for the Yorkshire under 11s programme and shares his insight on representative cricket for that age group.*

We at Skipton CC started a girls' section in the summer of 2021. There have been so many benefits to doing so, and the club has developed, grown and evolved over the last 12 months as a result.

More girls has meant more parent helpers, more female helpers, more friends and more fun.

Until we started actively attracting girls to the club in 2021, we had had very few at the club over the years. We used ECB funding to make an eight-week, girls-only Dynamos programme available for free for girls aged 8–11. As a result of sending this information to local primary schools, we had 25 girls join the course – an increase of 24 female junior players compared to the previous year.

With the help of some willing and enthusiastic volunteers, we delivered the Dynamos programme, based generally around the recommended activities, and we made it as much fun as possible. Energy and enthusiasm from coaches/helpers is a massive thing – they're infectious and I think are a big part of our success. If the coaches clearly love the game, the girls will be much more likely to love it too.

The girls themselves have loved it. They're so keen, and I always maintain that I could leave the cricket equipment out, not say anything, and they'd happily entertain themselves for two hours. I think that's a result of exposing the girls to a fun, relaxed cricket environment and the effect of motivated, inspiring coaches who love the game. I don't think the power of enthusiastic helpers can be underestimated, especially when working with this younger age group.

If the girls' first experience of cricket is one which is led by an engaging, positive adult whose love for cricket is infectious, they're much more likely to come back. As well as this, they're also more likely to tell their friends.

Music also helped, and we asked each girl to choose a song to add to our 'Dynamos playlist' that we played during training sessions. (Learn from my mistake and get access to a good sound system – my portable speaker works fine in a sports hall but definitely not on a cricket field!)

We made equipment easily visible and accessible for those who came early so they could just grab a bat and/or a ball and play before the session starts. This could be with another girl and/or with whichever adult they came with.

After the success of the Dynamos programme, we then gave any girls who wanted to continue playing half-price membership of the club, which included a free club playing shirt.

Since then, we've done a girls-only winter training programme. Out of the 25 girls who were with us in the summer of 2021, we've had 14 at the winter programme (and a few more who had other commitments and will join us in the summer), which is a retention rate we're really proud of.

Before we set up the winter training, we asked the girls' parents whether they wanted sessions to last one hour, one and a half hours, or two hours and whether they wanted it to last eight, 10 or 12 weeks. The results were almost unanimous, so we've just finished (April 2022) a 12-week programme of two hours per session.

This summer, we're one of four clubs that are going to be part of an inaugural U11 girls' league in our area. The league will be softball, and we at Skipton are also going to be taking part in softball festivals and hardball friendlies against other teams. On the subject of festivals, some of which we will be helping to organise and/or host, we're not excluding any clubs that don't have enough for a full team. The latest thinking is that we'll pool together at one venue all the girls from the area who want to play and split them into teams on the day. The aims are for them to play lots of cricket, have fun and make some new friends.

One more thing I'm going to do this year is to go into schools to deliver taster sessions. The schools will get one session for free, in exchange for my being able to give out flyers to promote the club. One of the flyers I'll give out is information about our girls' section, which will continue this year.

Alongside the girls' section, we have also started to offer women's cricket. It's really exciting to be part of something that is at the beginning of such inevitable exponential growth. We've found it difficult so far to recruit enough women, aside from the mums versus girls' games. I can't really share a success story for this (yet), but there are a few things we're trying and are going to try. For example, the league is developing editable online posters that can be personalised by clubs (to put their own club name, contact details, etc.) and posted on social media or in shops. I think this is a good idea because it means only one lot of 'work' is done, and it makes it easy for clubs to quickly edit a couple of boxes and then put them onto social media.

For spring/summer 2022, we've put on two training sessions for women – one hardball session alongside men's training and one softball session. Importantly, the softball training is at the same time as the girls. This means that mums (or other female carers) can play without having to worry about childcare – we're going to have all of them on the same pitch, with two different sessions running: one for women and one for girls.

The next step for us is to attract more secondary school-age girls to the club, so I'm going to go into local secondary schools to deliver cricket taster sessions in a bid to achieve this. Depending on their desire, ability and experience, they could join the women's group or the girls'.

Generally, it's really important to think about flexibility and what the barriers might be – for example, a lot of women and girls have a barrier to playing with a hardball (partly to do with all the padding up) and just want to turn up and have a social game of cricket.

Luckily, we haven't really encountered many problems. The clubs were, and continue to be, really supportive of women's and girls' cricket, and we are fortunate enough to have equal access to the ground for women's and girls' training and matches as the boys/men have. In addition to this, the club have willingly agreed to host Yorkshire girls' training sessions and matches.

One important thing to note is the mentality of us as adults involved in girls' cricket. Cricket for girls is only a big deal or 'not normal' if they're told it is. As a result of lots of hard work over the last few years, cricket is now much more accessible for women and girls. As adults, we probably grew up with men's cricket being much more popular and visible than women's game. To the girls of today, though, it's not a boys' sport – it's just *a* sport. Take The Hundred for example – if being introduced to that was a girl's first-ever experience of cricket, and you tried to tell her that cricket was a boys' sport, she'd probably think you were mad.

Yorkshire

Having worked with all of the Yorkshire girls' county age groups over the last couple of years and being the lead coach of the under-11s this year, I've also experienced the higher end of the talent pool of girls' cricket as well as those taking their very first steps in the sport.

Even at a county level, especially with the under-11s, we do a lot of softball as well as hardball cricket throughout the winter, to improve their game awareness and to get them thinking tactically. Just because they can play hardball cricket doesn't mean they can't still play with a softball too. There are skills to learn, and it can sometimes be seen as more 'fun' to play with a softball. It might also be more likely that they take risks and try things they might not with a hardball.

Thanks in large part to Rob Johnson (Women's and Girls' Club and League Development Manager in North and East Yorkshire, and the Yorkshire under-13 girls' coach), much of the winter under-11 and under-13 sessions this year involved lots of problem-solving and scenario-based games, most of which involved a softball. There have been lots of fun challenges thrown in too, like having to bat 'wrong-handed' or with an autograph bat, or scoring extra runs by doing a diving stop. As well as this, teams had 'superpowers', like the ability to remove all fielders or double the number of runs scored, for an over. All of this promoted lots of thinking and discussion and allowed for conversations that brought the girls closer together as friends as well as developing their cricket.

One final thing to finish on is the subject of cricket being a social sport, especially for girls. A great quote I once heard from Courtney Winfield-Hill (Senior Regional Talent Manager for the Northern Diamonds, and who assures me she heard the quote from someone else!) is that 'men/boys need to play well to belong, and women/girls need to belong to play well'. Partly with that in mind, I've done a couple of trips with my players so far – one with the Skipton girls to watch a women's T20 county match and one with the Yorkshire girls to go ten-pin bowling and for pizza. Both events went down well (with the girls and the parents), and I would recommend it as a way to build that social network that will help girls fulfil their potential as cricketers and, more importantly, as people.

Case Study: Hannah Stobbs: Coach, Player and Volunteer at Ickenham Cricket Club

Ickenham CC optimises what recreational sport is all about. They are one of many perfect examples of women's cricket clubs. Hannah Stobbs talks about how they built a thriving women's cricket section at the club from the ground up – including the challenges they faced along the way, as well as some of the most important aspects that contributed to their success on and off the pitch

How Did It All Start?

It all started, as it often does, with a group of friends who wanted to have a go at cricket. ICC Ladies started playing friendly fixtures in 2006 and joined the North London Women's League in 2009. The team won their first silverware (the North London T20 Cup) the following year and won the league for the first time in 2011. By this stage, some of the team were taking coaching badges and getting involved in supporting the growing girls' section. ICC Ladies are hugely proud that two of the girls who came through the girls' setup are Sunrisers and Middlesex 1st XI players Katie Wolfe and Emily Thorpe. ICC Ladies joined the Southern League in 2014 and worked their way up to the Premier League in 2019 after back-to-back promotions.

What were the key things you needed to have in place to get started?

A desire to learn, a good sense of fun, a growth mind set, a willingness to overcome barriers and strong communication and teamwork to navigate the admin and the red tape.

What are the key things now that help the team operate (on and off the pitch)?

We have maintained our good sense of humour and fun. Our number one priority is to enjoy our cricket as we are a group of friends first and foremost and cricketers second. Outside of cricket, we have turned our hand to escape rooms, tours, Eton Fives, running clubs including marathons and half marathons, darts and many more. We have a core group of organisers who set up open lines of communication and work hard to ensure everyone enjoys their time at Ickenham CC, with plenty of opportunities to grow as players and as people. We also take a community-based approach to running the club and run 'Ickenham Sixes' 6-aside league/tournament both indoors and outdoors to build bridges with other clubs in Middlesex and beyond. We love the competitive and friendly nature that this approach fosters and always look forward to playing against other local clubs. We aim to use our social media platforms to showcase positive role models to the wider cricketing world and we enjoyed putting together some short videos for Women's Cricket Chat and for International Women's Day in the 2022 winter pre-season. In 2022, we are looking to extend our provision beyond two women's teams and re-establish our U-11 and U-13 girls setup at the club. We look forward to more growth in the years to come as we continue to enjoy our cricket.

How do you cater for differences in abilities?

ICC Ladies XI plays in the WCSL Championship (2021–present) and, due to the exponential growth of women's cricket at the club in recent years, ICC Ladies were in the position to enter their 2XI team into the Middlesex Derek Morgan League in 2021. This means that players have the opportunity to give cricket a go for the very first time, grow as a player in a supportive setup or play a competitive standard of cricket. Thanks to the excellent leadership of our captains, there are plenty of opportunities for county players and those wishing to make it into the regional systems to not only grow their main skill but also develop their second and third skills. This strengthens them as players and in turn helps with county and regional selection (it's not unusual for our promising young opening bowlers to be promoted up the batting order to test their skills under pressure!)

How do you negotiate the use of facilities with the men's part of the club?

We have a Women's Cricket Rep on the main club committee which helps to keep lines of communication open with the club as a whole.

We are very fortunate to have the Men's 1XI Captain coaching us (as of January 2022) as we wanted to have more organised training sessions to further the development of our players. The door is open for us to play in the men's teams, and some of our players have enjoyed taking up that opportunity. All of these things help the men at the club to develop an understanding of women's cricket and the space we need to reach our full potential.

Top tips for clubs wanting to set up their own women's team:

First and foremost, cricket is there to be enjoyed. Keep fun and humour at the heart of all you do as you navigate the hurdles or obstacles you may face when you set up your team. Second, keep communicating with your team, your club and your county board. There are plenty of people out there who can advise and help you, provide access to funding or give you the opportunities that you need. Finally, be ambitious and remind yourselves that you can achieve all that you set out to – you will be pleasantly surprised at how quickly a small idea (with a healthy dose of courage to put yourself out there) can grow into a full team, or two!

CHAPTER SUMMARY

- Building the foundations from the bottom up is crucial
- Female players should have the same access to facilities and equipment as male players
- Develop strong links with local schools or clubs
- Create an environment that caters for both serious and social players

CHAPTER 3

Coaching Female Cricketers and Teams

You can split coaching into different levels from beginner/recreational, through to club cricket, county age groups, county cricket, the regional structures, The Hundred and then to the England Academy and U19 Team through to the senior England team. Coaching at each of these levels requires a different emphasis.

For recreational players who might be starting the game for the very first time, it's really important for them to have female role models at the club they're involved with. Having male coaches who understand what it's like to work with young girls is great and will always be really important. That said, clubs should put a lot of emphasis on encouraging and training female coaches. This will have a marked effect on attracting young girls to the club and have them stay there for the long term.

Insight: Ebony Rainford-Brent – Broadcaster and Former England Cricketer

I'd love to see an increase in elite female coaches. We're starting to see signs of this, but it isn't enough. It'd be great to see more women believing that they can reach the top levels of coaching and working towards it.

Insight: Kevin Gresham, Coach Development Manager, Yorkshire

Over the last three to four years, the aim has been to develop young female coaches to work with the county age group (CAG) girls both on the winter programmes and during the summer. All these coaches have come through the CAG system themselves so have relatable experiences and can add value to the player journey.

These young coaches are mentored by more experienced members of the coaching team. The female game is evolving rapidly with a recognisable structure being put into place so the need for coaches who are committed to female cricket is vital. Hopefully, we are now seeing coaches who understand the pathway and what is required to support and develop players at all levels.

Coaches need to be prepared to go that little bit further for the players to get to know them as people so they can understand the pressures that teenage girls experience in all parts of life. Cricket sessions need to be safe, inclusive environments from a social view as much as from a game development view.

We can't ever stop trying to improve the player's game, that is why they want to be selected for county programmes, but we can't improve them if they are not feeling comfortable in their surroundings.

At the recreational level, the first thing a club should ask itself is 'what is the players' reason for turning up to the club?'. Often it's simply a case of them enjoying being around other girls of a similar age in a social setting. They might not necessarily be driven by getting better at cricket; it may just be a chance for them to be active, chat and laugh with friends. With this in mind, clubs should do everything they can to foster a fun environment. We often use music during training sessions, fun games, haribo breaks and such things, to make sure those that are there purely for fun will have exactly that.

Insight: Lisa Keightley – Former England Head Coach and Former Australian Cricketer

When I was coaching Junior girls we wanted a nice, relaxed, have-fun environment. I think the players respond really well to having a good time with their mates.

The skill level varies so much in underage girls' cricket. So for me, it was always keeping the good players engaged, keeping the player that was a little bit underpowered also engaged. And then, the ones in the middle were easy, because they were happy to do the real basic stuff and excited to move on. But for me, I just kept it really game-based. I used to teach one or two skills per session, and then they go into games and make it fun and get them to laugh. That way, I felt that they all enjoyed what they did. I didn't put any pressure on them. If we won or lost I didn't care, as long as they left laughing and having a good time.

There'll then be those players who join a club with a strong motivation to improve at cricket, to progress through the ranks and to take pride and enjoyment in their development.

As a coach, it's important to strike the balance between catering to these two separate motivations. There should be a fun environment for those there for that, as well as being able to push and develop the really keen girls. The good news is that it's perfectly possible to do both.

I know from being coached myself, when starting something relatively new, you always want that positive reinforcement. Without this, there's a danger that players can become disengaged really quickly. The language you use as a coach is vital to this. You'll be able to see that a player might be making mistakes or doing something incorrectly, and it's how you respond to this that will have a big impact on player engagement levels. Try to build positivity in every interaction and use phrases like 'Your effort is great and you're making great progress, have you thought about trying to do it like this?'. This is far more effective than simply pointing out the mistakes and telling them what they should be doing instead.

Insight: Lisa Keightley, Former England Head Coach and Former Australian Cricketer

If players look bored and disengaged, I think about how I can set up the session a bit differently to get the engagement. What I found is if they're learning a new skill, or they're trying to improve their game, you get that engagement. You get the player at their best when giving players choices, not always setting up the session that you want. A lot of times I'll put three options up for a player. And I ask what do you want to do today? And they would give me a choice, and I run with that. In that way, I find they buy into the session because they've had a choice.

The historical inequalities for the women's and girls' game have led to a large variation in the skill levels of the players. In the boys' game, the setup will likely have long-established teams of under-8s, under-9s, under-10s and all the way up to under-17s, leading to a constant production line of players with experience and higher ability. The girls' game hasn't had that benefit of mass participation in the same way, so clubs might have an under-11s team, then it skips an age group up to under-13s, then to under-15s and under-17s. For a lot of clubs, the difference can be even more vast. Some may have an under-13s group that might have to cater to a ten-year-old girl, all the way up to a teenage girl. Following this, there may only be a jump up to under-17s, with a 14-year-old playing with 17-year-olds. This can and does create a mismatch of ability and experience levels in the same groups, which is a big challenge for a coach.

To manage this, I'd suggest using a lot of circuit sessions. As an example, if you were doing a particular drill, you might split a set of 20 players into smaller groups of 5. You can then be really clear in your groupings, by having the more advanced girls together, then with every group matched on the basis of ability levels, including a softball group if needed. Then for each of the four stations of the drill, each set of players moves around and the coach can adapt the drill to suit the individual needs. As an example, if you were teaching the front-foot drive at one station, you might have the batters aiming to hit the ball through a specific area. For the less experienced, you could have them hitting the ball from a tee, then each ability level can be catered for with drop feeds, bobble feeds or actual overarm throws with a hardball.

The ability groupings can be diplomatically difficult for a coach to decide, but in general, the players will likely say if they feel like they're being undersold or oversold in terms of ability. It's also worth remembering that if a player would prefer to be in a higher or lower ability level group then that's absolutely fine to switch around where necessary. It could also be as simple as having both tennis balls and cricket balls at each station and asking the player if they have a preference. There's clearly a safety element in that if you know for sure a girl isn't ready to play hardball cricket, then you can just be completely honest with them and say so. This can also be framed as a positive, whereby you can give them a challenge. You might say that if they achieved certain things by the end of the session then they can move on to hardball the following week. To reemphasise this point, you can see the difference between this in comparison to simply saying 'you're not ready for hardball cricket'.

IS IT DIFFERENT FROM COACHING FEMALE PLAYERS TO MALE PLAYERS?

Insight: Charlotte Edwards CBE, Coach and Former England Captain

One thing I've learned now going into coaching is that I treat everyone really separately: in terms of they're just people, and they're just cricketers.

But there are some subtle differences in what you might find as a coach. With girls' cricket, the ball isn't as quick, so I think it is more of a front-foot game, and you've got to create more power.

The girls generally need pushing to believe in themselves more than the boys. The boys, if you ask them to play a reverse sweep, they'll just go and play it, and they'll know how to do it. Where I think with the girls, you've probably got to make them play it. And then they realise they're actually really good at it. So, they're not necessarily going to put themselves out there as much as boys. But I'm not saying that's a bad thing, either. So, boys, you sometimes have to hold back, girls, you've got to push forward. And as a coach, I think that's the great thing about coaching, everyone's different. And some girls are more confident than others. So, it's just understanding them as players before you really start to coach the specifics.

This is perhaps the question we're asked most often when we're talking about coaching women's and girls' cricket. Clearly, it isn't a question that can be discussed in absolute terms, and there'll always be exceptions to the rules. It's also impossible to answer without using generalisations of some form. Good coaches get to know the players they work with, so individualised coaching should always be emphasised above the notion that boys learn one way and girls learn another. That said, there are certainly things to consider when coaching girls over boys.

Insight: Adam Collins, Journalist and Broadcaster

There's a growing group of people that are seeing women's cricket almost as a different game from men's cricket. The absence of raw pace and raw power has meant the game has to be more technical, and the players need a bigger bag of tricks. Players have to work the ball through the gaps rather than look to bludgeon constantly. This isn't at the exclusion of power in the women's game. The fact that it's more distinctive makes it more of an event, unlike the men's game where pure power is now just the norm and seeing three sixes in a row isn't as exciting as it once was.

First, we need to remember that boys tend to watch more cricket from an early age, whether that be live in stadiums or on TV. In general, girls likely haven't watched as much as boys, and this means coaches shouldn't necessarily assume their knowledge levels are the same. At the introductory level, young girls mightn't have comparable knowledge of the tactical elements of the game, so this should be taken into consideration and a higher emphasis put on gameplay over tactics at the beginner level. Having had some really interesting chats with many male coaches who work in clubs historically with boys' teams and who are now working with the girls' teams, this is one of the common challenges they speak about. They often assume knowledge from the players purely because they expect the girls to have watched a lot more cricket than the boys. This is not a negative or a positive, it is just something that is helpful for coaches and teachers to be aware of – some terminologies may need more explanation or clarity. No doubt as the game progresses and as girls' cricket continues to become more mainstream, this challenge is likely to fade away or not be as prominent as it is now.

Girls and boys can mature at different rates, and we often find that girls can show increased emotional intelligence at an early age. They can be more sensitive* to their teammates and can appreciate a little more what their friends are going through, whereas boys tend to be more likely to just plough on with each other. This means a girl's coach would need to show a little more of a compassionate side when working with the players, whereas a boy's coach can be more direct with them and give them more instant feedback. With the girls, we should be more compassionate and give them a bit more of a cushion with the feedback you give them. We try to make sure we always include positive points around any corrections to what they're doing, both before and after the 'negative'. There's a well-known sandwich metaphor that many of you will be familiar with at this stage that isn't entirely appropriate for a book!

*I would like to emphasise that we are by no means feeding into the often frustrating narrative that females are over-sensitive and too emotional in certain environments. Far from it, having high levels of emotional intelligence and empathy for others is an absolute super strength and should be looked upon as that in my humble opinion!

Ultimately, at the recreational level, it's about a coach asking themselves, 'how can I make this session the most positive experience possible for the girls?' It isn't always about (although in some cases it absolutely can and should be) how can I make them a better cricketer. As the levels progress, this can and should change, but it is something to be mindful of when coaching younger girls who are new to the game.

Insight: Lisa Keightley, Former England Head Coach and Former Australian Cricketer

I try to empower the player with confidence and belief, and not to strip it away. Sometimes, if you lose, it's really easy to strip that confidence and belief away. When teams lose that's your biggest challenge. It's quite easy to yell and scream. But that's not my style. It's about trying to bring out the confidence and give them confidence, rather than take it away.

Another difference we see is the amount of older girls/women (we'd normally use 18+ as a slightly vague age guideline) taking up cricket at the recreational level, something we see less of in the men's game with it being more historically well established and supported. We've found that while recreational women players still enjoy the social aspect of the game, they're also more driven to get better. As a coach, you can be more prescriptive and directional with your style of delivery than you'd need to be with younger girls. They actively want to be coached on what they're not doing correctly and learn how to get better. Coaches can and should adapt to this after they've established this is the players' motivation for being there.

As mentioned earlier, language is incredibly important to discuss when looking at the difference in coaching females and males; it's also a pretty straightforward thing to address. To feel entirely included and welcome in a sport is key to a player of any gender to maintain enjoyment and motivation. Small changes can make a genuine difference, and we've seen this recently with the welcome guidelines to use the term 'batter' instead of 'batsman'. This might seem minor, and more 'old school' cricket followers have questioned whether it really matters. It certainly does to the young girls coming into the sport who simply want to feel like it's a sport for everyone. Think of a young boy coming into cricket and how it might change their motivation if the accepted term had always been 'batswoman'.

The language around role models is also important. We have so many fantastic male coaches at the recreational level that give so much to the sport but have grown up almost exclusively with the men's game as their point of reference. That can often lead to examples used by coaches referring to male players, when coaching female players. If a girl starts to learn to swing the ball, they might hear comparisons to Jimmy Anderson, or a good batter might hear Virat Kohli or Joe Root. While they're meant as compliments and with good intentions, it makes a real difference for girls to hear female examples. As a coach of female players, I'd encourage you to watch the women's game so you can use examples like Katherine Brunt, Meg Lanning or Marizanne Kapp. Don't underestimate the significance of the difference these kind of changes makes. Young girls aren't aspiring to be male players; they're aspiring to be female players, so try to harness their aspirations accordingly.

TECHNICAL DIFFERENCES

While many technical elements of the female and male games are essentially the same with regard to what you coach, there are some that need different emphases.

Insight: Charlotte Edwards CBE, Coach and Former England Captain

For batters, hitting the ball straight and hard would probably be the one thing I'd coach from a really early age with girls; getting a bat coming through straight and not thinking that their power is with their bottom hand across the line. Being able to judge the length I think is probably one of the biggest challenges I find, being able to adapt from playing front and back foot and doing it quickly and judging that length are key.

That's one thing I'm constantly talking about judging the length well, and we hit the ball hard and straight. It's simple, isn't it, sometimes, cricket!

I think with bowlers, you want to encourage them to bowl the ball fast because I think their natural reaction is to try to put the ball there on the spot. So, encourage them and recognise and reward them for doing that. So, everything they do is really positive; we want to do it the best way we possibly can.

With fielding, that's the biggest area I think we can influence in terms of the drills we set up for them, and how we want our players to be athletic, diving really early on, so they do not fear. There are lots of things you can do. And making the fielding sessions really intense rather than just laid back and going through the motions, I think is something that has really worked well with us.

Generally speaking, boys and girls tend to do different activities when they're growing up that have different outcomes for their physical development. Boys can be more active in terms of climbing trees or playing unorganised/informal sports in their spare time. If they were at the beach it's more likely boys will pick up pebbles and throw them into the sea than girls. While a horrible stereotype that I'm hesitant to use, there's some truth in it. This means that boys' physical development can be different from that of girls. When coming to playing cricket for the first time, a lot of these basic skills are therefore different. Again, this is not a negative or a positive, it is simply acknowledging that girls and boys can often have different exposures and environments when growing up which can impact different skills within cricket.

The biggest thing I see in an overall sense is that the throwing capability of boys is much more advanced than girls from a young age. From a coaching point of view, you therefore need to spend more time coaching the girls how to throw. It's a case of breaking down the entire throwing technique from the last point (flicking the wrist), to getting their elbow above shoulder height, to bringing their shoulder all the way back. There's a video on the cricket for girls website https://cricketforgirls.com/ that explains this.

The other big difference is with the girls' batting. I've seen that girls tend to worry more about getting out, so they can have less focus on one of the fun parts of batting, hitting the ball hard. As a result of this, their backswing can be less than you see from boys at an early age. I'd advise to spend more time on getting their setup correct, so they can develop the higher backswing needed to hit the ball harder. You can do this by removing the stumps during a drill, so you take away the consequence of missing the ball. Then really encourage them to take a high backswing and hit the ball much harder.

Insight: Charlotte Edwards CBE, Coach and Former England Captain

The most important person is the player, so I think you've got to sit them down, you've got to explain the pros and cons of what's happening. And ultimately, it's up to them. If they don't buy into it, we may as well not go any further. I'm very much of the philosophy that it's player led. I'll give you all the information, I'll share all my thoughts with you in a constructive way, but you've got to make the change. Because if you don't want to make the change, you're not going to do it. So, all the players I work with, it's done on that basis. You just lay out the pros and cons. You show them some video and off we go. So, I try and do it in a very simple way, and not confrontational for them as well. And I think when you've got those fundamentals that you're trying to work to, they understand it even more than that you want to hit straight. Say, with batting, if you have got a grip problem, then you're going to understand that more because we want you to hit the ball straight. So, I think it all should follow suit. But it's definitely down to the player.

The difference in natural power from boys to girls is also important to think about when coaching batting. I played most of my formative years as a cricketer against boys and would often see their mis-hit shots go for six because of their added physicality. A mis-hit for a female player is more likely to be skied and caught. This leads to two key points that a coach should focus on. First, the emphasis on female batters hitting into the gaps. They need to be more precise with where they're hitting the ball so there's a very real conclusion that the female game needs to be more skilful than the male. As a coach, set up targets, be really clear as to how they can work the ball into those targets and emphasise technique and skill in order to do so. This links to the second point. Female players' techniques have to be immaculate when moving into performance levels. Really encourage them to see the importance of regular tennis ball drills. There can be a perception of tennis ball drills that they're boring and players just want to hit hard balls, but they're so important at every level of the game. It's our job as coaches to make these drills exciting and fun so players maintain enthusiasm for doing them. Rather than just simply doing drop feeds, add targets, make it a competition, anything to increase the engagement levels. This is also where coaches see who's willing to spend time doing these drills because they know it makes a big difference to their technique, compared to those that don't. You'll find it's a good indicator of what their motivation is for being there (fun vs improvement).

Insight: Lisa Keightley, Former England Head Coach and Former Australian Cricketer

If you asked me a question ten years ago, I'd say technique is really important because we don't have the raw strength. I thought that if you are technically sound and you're using your body the best way it can, you can get every bit of power out of it. But I'd say now, in the more professional era, the players are getting stronger, faster, and fitter. If you look at Sophia Dunkley, the way she holds a bat, I don't think ten years ago I'd have been trying to get her hands together, I'd be thinking, well, she needs to get the most out of a body, she needs to have a whip at the end. Now that she's stronger and more powerful, and the bats are better, the boundaries become smaller, she can clear the boundary. She hits it as hard as anyone so I'm more inclined to leave subtle personal preference a little bit alone unless they don't have power. I still think you need a pretty good base around your technique. And it can't be so out there that you have really big weaknesses. You need, I'd say 80–20. If you've got 80% of the basics pretty good and sound, I'd be happy with 20% that might look a little bit different.

With bowling, this can also be a victim of many girls not having seen as much cricket on TV as boys. They might need extra work on bowling with a straight arm and I'd suggest not having them too far away from each other at the early ages when bowling. Being closer to the target builds up their confidence and stops the development of throwing instead of bowling. You can then gradually move it further apart as their confidence grows.

Insight: Lisa Keightley, Former England Head Coach and Former Australian Cricketer

I still think you need really good foundations and technical ability through your bowling action to get that most out of your body, even though the players are getting stronger and fitter. I still think, if someone comes through with a braced front leg, they're going to be quicker than most that don't.

MOVING UP THROUGH THE LEVELS

There's a shift in emphasis as a coach when players start to progress in ability. The motivation of the player is likely to be moving more towards improvement so your coaching should reflect this. You can now begin to increase the amount of instructional coaching, still with an emphasis on enjoyment and a two-way conversation, but you can start being more direct in your feedback. If you're working with a talented player and you don't think they're performing as well as you think they can, you can say this, you can get more technical with them and work with them to nurture their aspirations. You can still be positive in this feedback and use phrases like 'you're much better than what you're showing today'.

One of the common mistakes we see with coaching females is coaches *constantly* giving feedback. In my experience it's certainly noticeable that girls will listen more than boys. While this is a great trait to have, it can also lead to coaches (particularly at the county age group and club level) thinking that the more the player listens intently, the more the coach wants to speak. This can inevitably lead to information overload and becomes more of a hindrance than a help. Using too much information can discourage a player from taking ownership of their own game and subsequently become too reliant on the coach. I've experienced this myself, when batting in a net with a coach doing throwdowns to me. The coach didn't give me an opportunity to share how I was feeling in terms of my technique; they just peppered me with feedback and I struggled with this. They were trying to coach me as a left-handed batter on playing off spin bowling, with the ball turning away from me. When the ball dropped shorter, my natural reaction was to rock onto the back foot and look to punch through the off-side. The coach wanted me to go onto the back foot and hit hard through the leg side instead. This is a huge change in technique and emphasis and I never had the chance to explain how unnatural this felt as it was just a one-way conversation. You should still try to focus on one or two technical points in a session, no matter how much you think the player listening and nodding to you means they want more. Try to hold yourself back! Also remember to keep asking the player how things feel for them if you're working on a different technique, players need to have a level of ownership of their own game.

When players then progress up to the high-performance level, there's more subtle differences that coaches should take into consideration.

First, I'd say that females really like to know what a session is going to entail. This might be a week or a day in advance, but the more you can communicate what's actually going to happen at forthcoming sessions the better. Some coaches aren't naturally organised and have some excellent sessions mapped out in their own heads, but communicating these in advance is definitely preferable when coaching at this level. Of course, sometimes players have to be flexible and just roll with things, but in my experience, female players like to feel as prepared as possible before going into a session, more so than male players.

I wanted to use my own cricketing journey to describe what good (and bad) coaching can look like. At county age group level, I was lucky enough to have a fantastic coach. He had a deep passion for the game that was incredibly infectious. If he saw someone do something good he'd make a big deal of it and praised us enthusiastically. If you were that player it felt great and if you weren't, you wanted to be. He had a really nice way of pointing out mistakes, often by making a light-hearted joke about it. He wouldn't do it in a mickey taking way, more in a caring way as he'd built up such good relationships with the players he worked with.

On the flip side, I've seen coaches who hadn't put any emphasis on developing positive relationships with players; it was much more of a stern, 'I talk, you listen' style. They'd go straight in and simply started pointing out mistakes, which is never the way to achieve the best results with players and leads to their disengagement.

Insight: Heather Knight OBE, England Captain

I've been lucky to have worked with a coach that only spoke when he felt like he needed to add something, and I quite like that approach to coaching; it enabled me to dictate what I wanted to do and think for myself about how I wanted to develop. He'd point me in the right direction and add things, but I felt like I was in charge of my own learning, my own practice, and I think that's quite an important thing that young cricketers need to develop. Quite often, you get dictated to quite a lot, and you almost become reliant on someone else telling you what to do or become reliant on someone else forming a plan for you.

When you play cricket, you're out there on your own, and you have to adapt and find your own way of doing things and be able to think for yourself. I think that's quite an important thing that coaches can do to develop self-awareness and game awareness for players when they do go out, and they don't have to have that super amount of direction and to be able to have to deal with things.

At the heart of coaching lies relationship building. Yes, having good technical knowledge is important, but if you don't have the trust of the player then the technical information won't be absorbed.

It all comes back to what the motivation of player is for being there and what you can do as a coach to nurture this.

I wanted to end this chapter with a case study based on the research of Dr Stuart McErlain-Naylor, who has looked specifically at the differences in male and female batters. It's really interesting to note the subtle differences and what they might mean for coaching.

Case study: Dr Stuart McErlain-Naylor

Can you give a general overview of the research you carried out?

I think the thing that came out most strongly when we were actually writing it up was the idea that male and female cricket are not the same. I think that was almost a starting point. Because I think before you compare male and female differences in anything, you almost need to justify, well, why is there a need to compare the two? How do you know it's not just height difference, or it's not just strength difference? Why is it a gender difference? I think the more we started to think about it, we say sporting technique is genuinely influenced by three things. It's the individual person, the task they've got to do and the environment that they're in. All three of those things are different for male and female cricket, especially for batting that we looked at specifically.

When we started to think about it, it is things like, for the individual, height and limb length will be different, which then might potentially lead to a different technique being ideal.

We can't just say we've done loads of research on male batting and now this is how you should go and coach all cricketers everywhere. Because a bit like we say you can't just coach children like young adults, and they need specific coaching advice, the same applies for female sport.

But it's very under-researched. You've got limb length, height, body mass and strength. All of these things are different, which might mean that the best way for a male with regard to power hitting the ball as far as possible might not be the best way for a female to hit the ball as far as possible.

When you start thinking about equipment, the ball is a different size and mass, which is going to influence the impact. The bat is a different size and mass. All of these things mean that if you gave a male – a power hitting specialist – a female bat, the optimum technique might change because they're swinging a different thing through the air.

I think the bit I found the most interesting, personally, was when we started to think about a task itself, because the boundary is shorter in female cricket, and so even the task of hitting a six is a different requirement. Instead of saying your task is to clear this boundary, the moment you change where that boundary is, there then becomes a trade off in speed/accuracy. In most sports, the moment you try to become more accurate, you'll trade off some speed. In football, if you wanted to just kick the ball as hard as possible, if you then said we need you to hit it within this target, they'd trade off some speed to make sure they can be more accurate. If you say, in cricket, if we want you to clear a boundary that's not quite as far, they might be able to use a different technique that's more accurate but less powerful. And so the recommendation changes from 'you've got to do it really fast, so use this technique', to 'you've got to hit it kind of far, but you can use this technique because it's more accurate, or there's more margin for error'. But then when you think about the incoming ball speed being different, it means that actually what we've done in the past, like a study we did on male power hitting where we had players ranging from club players all the way through to senior England internationals, we said, what do the best people that are able to hit the ball further do differently in their technique, and how can we provide recommendations for coaching based on that?

We think there's a solid justification for why that may not apply to women, because it's essentially a different task done by different people in a different environment.

What did you find on the male side of things in the research that you did? Were there any notable things that came out of it?

There were 20 males or so, roughly an even spread of club players and elite players. We basically said, against the bowling machine – so everyone was getting the same delivery, hit the ball as far as you can.

Then we collated the statistics to say what things predict greater ball carry distance. Of the three things that came out, the most important was something we call X-factor, which is from golf research, which is the separation between your hips and your shoulders.

The way I normally illustrate it is if you draw a line through your hips, from left to right hip, and a line through your shoulders, if you rotate both things together, they're just going to stay together and move. It's not just the rotation; it's how much you can separate them. If you can almost leave your hips behind and rotate your shoulders further, that then stretches all the muscles in your chest so that they can recoil and impart more force into the arms and the back.

We found that people who were able to separate their hips and shoulders, and rotate more, hit the ball further. That was the most important predictor that we found.

The second most important thing was lead elbow extension, that is, the front arm. The players that were able to hit the ball further extended their elbow during the downswing. So to start the downswing with a flexed elbow, and then by the time they hit the ball, their elbow would be straight, whereas the people who didn't hit it as far, did that less.

Then the final and third thing was wrist uncocking, which is essentially just the wrist. Again, I think that comes from golf and baseball research, where we're talking about cocking and uncocking the wrist during the swing.

The order of importance was starting at the centre of the body and then going downwards. The hips and shoulders were the most important, followed by the elbow, and then the wrist. It builds on this idea of you generating all the momentum and energy through the centre of the body, that you then transfer it through the arms into the bat.

It's a bit like stuff I've done before in vertical jumping, just saying jump as high as you can. Generally, people will straighten their hips, then their knees, then their ankles last and it travels down the body in what we'd call a kinetic chain. It's the same thing in male power hitting. So, separate the hips and the shoulders, extend the elbow and then the wrist at the end.

The way we generally work in research is we'll use previous studies to form our hypothesis that we'll then test in subsequent studies. Because we obviously expected that male batters would swing the bat faster and hit the ball further than females based on everything we knew to that date, we hypothesised that those three things I just said would be different between males and females.

What did you find when comparing males and female players?

We tested 15 women that ranged from club to elite international players which we then paired with 15 of the men from the existing data.

I think, probably as you'd expect, the male batters swung the bat faster, they then hit the ball faster, and the ball travelled a further distance. But then the interesting bit becomes, well, why did that happen?

The main thing that came out was by far the biggest differences were all at the elbow, so both lead and rear elbows. The biggest differences were all in the lead elbow around that second thing I mentioned earlier of elbow extension. Whereas the males were extending that elbow during the downswing, the females, on average, actually flexed their elbow – only by a few degrees.

It's probably more accurate to think of it as keeping the elbow still rather than flexing it, because it was only a few degrees on average. But they were basically keeping the elbow flexed the whole way through.

When we looked into what does that actually look like, we were basically saying that they're using more of a checked drive rather than a specific power hitting technique.

I think a lot of the men have developed a specific technique that's possibly high risk, high reward for how do we maximise power hitting. Whereas it seems like the female batters are using the same techniques that they've developed through their career, more of a traditional cricket shot, and just trying to play it faster rather than switching to a different technique, which, again, you can argue, is it due to strength? Is it that they're not strong enough to use the technique that the men are using? Is it that through either funding resources or coaching that they've just not been coached to do anything differently for power hitting? Or, again, this is what we don't know the answer to but where I get really interested, is it actually that the technique they're using is actually the best one for them?

If you can hit the ball for six, there's absolutely no incentive in cricket for you to hit the ball further. Therefore, this is again when we don't have answers like I say, but it's where I found it really interesting was to say, if by coaching these women to use the same techniques the men are using, if they can hit the ball further, but they've got less control over it, or there's less margin for error, then actually, is that a worse technique for them?

Would you rather have them actually not hit it as far but still clear the boundary, and they've got more control, more margin for error in terms of if you mistime it slightly, what happens? If you can mistime it slightly and it's still a good shot, then that's really important. Whereas if in the power hitting technique, if you mistime it slightly, it's going to loop up in the air and you get caught. Or you mistime it and you've missed the ball, then actually, is that speed/accuracy trade-off or are the female players occupying a different area in that speed/accuracy space, where they can't hit it quite as far, but they've got more control over it?

What are the main takeaways for coaches from your research?

I definitely wouldn't recommend you switch to using the technique that we found that males used. But I also wouldn't say we've seen that elite female batters are using this technique, therefore, we should coach all girls to use that technique. I think what I would say is that if they haven't previously, players and coaches should be encouraged to explore the alternatives in terms of play around with the weight of the bat and see what happens. They should also be encouraged to try different techniques, especially around the elbow in terms of keeping it flexed or extending it. If you haven't previously done any power hitting specific coaching, then play around with hitting the ball in different ways and see what happens. And even if we did have all the answers, I believe that coaching is almost encouraging players to explore and find their own movement solutions. Each player has a different size and strength, and so their optimum technique will be different to everyone else's. It's always a good recommendation to just explore what works for that person. But I think rather than concrete 'you should do this', my advice would be that based on conversations I've had, it seems there's been relatively little exploration of power hitting training, specifically in certain aspects of female cricket. Explore what specific effect it has and for that athlete and come to your own conclusions.

If you work with multiple players, you can start to get a feel for how the physically stronger players respond well to this training. While the bowlers who are batting lower down the order should stick with the check drives that they're using. But on the top opening batter we can work on specific interventions, either based on strength training, separating the hips and the shoulders or just swinging down and straightening their elbow into the ball strike. A bit of a politician's answer, but I'd say, is to encourage people to explore and try alternatives, if they haven't been doing previously.

CHAPTER SUMMARY

- Emphasise the training and development of female coaches
- Build in positivity to every interaction
- Good coaches get to know the players they work with
- Keep language inclusive

CHAPTER 4

How to Develop Mentally Strong Cricketers

WHAT DO WE MEAN BY MENTAL STRENGTH?

Before we define mental strength, it's important to emphasise the various ways in which mentality in cricket is discussed. We often hear terms like mental toughness, mental strength, positivity, a 'can do' attitude, a 'tough cookie', grit, determination and a whole host of others. All of these have their places and are used interchangeably (as I'll use interchangeably throughout the chapter), but it's also worth considering terms like mental agility or mental flexibility. Sport psychology is an increasingly important element across all sports and examines all of these and more. While this isn't designed to be an academic sport psychology chapter, it *is* designed to provoke thoughts around the mentality of cricketers and how you can enhance it.

It is often suggested that success in cricket is attributed to 90% mental and 10% physical skills. Like most sports, many coaches and players claim that the only difference between those who 'make it' and those who don't is simply down to their mental toughness. People's skill levels can be exactly the same, but it is players who are 'mentally tough' who go on and experience the highs and lows of elite sport.

Insight: Charlotte Edwards CBE, Coach and Former England Captain

Playing boys' cricket helped the mental side of the game for me. I think it's really important. I don't think I would have had the career I had if I had not played boys' cricket. It taught me so many things. It made me more resilient as a player. It made me deal with difficult situations which I came across quite a lot when I was growing up. So, it definitely made me a tougher cricketer. I don't know if that's a good thing or a bad thing because it can put off some girls. So, I think you have to be really careful and look at the character of the player to see if they can deal with playing boys' cricket or men's cricket. If they don't, that's fine; they go down the women's avenue. But I think there are a lot of benefits from playing boys' and men's cricket.

My toughness was formed because I had no other option if I'm honest. I had to put myself in those situations because I loved playing cricket. And I love playing cricket; therefore, my only avenue to play it was playing boys' and men's cricket. And it was horrible, I'm not going to shy away from that. Turning up and not being accepted, and often being sniggered at for being a girl. My desire and passion to play cricket far outweigh their negative comments towards me. I wouldn't want to put another girl through what I went through, but it made me bloody tough. And now I'm trying to find ways in my coaching; how do I get girls as tough as that? But then I think it's the way the sessions you put them through, and not letting them back out, and keep pushing until you can hopefully find the right level. It's hard, you can be tough, but also make them enjoy the game. So, it's a really difficult balance, but certainly possible.

Players are encouraged to spend time developing their physical skills, honing their techniques and getting fitter. More recently people have started to pay more attention to the psychological aspect of the game. The good thing is players of any age or ability can develop mental toughness and also learn to understand and combat how they feel in pressured situations.

Insight: Lisa Keightley, Former England Head Coach and Former Australian Cricketer

Resilience comes from experience, understanding why you felt like you did and working out a few strategies to help.

Mike Rotherham is a leading sport psychologist in the United Kingdom who has worked with Olympic athletes at the English Institute of Sport as well as with the England Women's Cricket Team. Mike was the sport psychologist when England's women won the 2017 World Cup at Lord's versus India.

Mike explains what he feels makes up mental toughness:

Toughness comes in many forms. The ability to; bounce back from setbacks; keep going in the face of difficult circumstances; the ability to take the tough (but right) decision (e.g., injury rehab and not giving in to peer pressures); perform under pressure; stay focused on the right things that will help performance.

If we analyse this, mental toughness encompasses many things, and it would seem that those who excel are the ones who continue to thrive even when things get hard. It is players who are open to feeling uncomfortable, to being in situations they know they may not always succeed in and who will not let things deter them from getting back up when they have been knocked down.

An area that has limited information is how and if mental toughness is different when it comes to female players compared to male players.

This next section comes with a *very* clear health warning! The observations are meant as general, not specific. Good coaches, parents, teachers and everyone else involved with sports know that athletes are individuals. They shouldn't be pigeonholed as a 'male' or 'female' athlete with regard to their psychology. The observations made by Mike are based on *some* experiences, and he himself acknowledges fully that they aren't meant as cut-and-dried theories. They're there to provoke thought rather than stereotype and should be treated as such.

We will go on to analyse the observations Mike has made and explain how coaches, teachers, players and parents can use this information to their benefit.

> *Females are generally more coachable and open to ideas and perspectives. Males, you sometimes have to get past their ego before being able to do any work.*

While a stereotype, this is a nice characteristic to have when a player is continually searching for new ways to get better and improve. It provides players with opportunity to explore and develop new skills and ideas; however, it is extremely important to point out the importance of how coaches use this knowledge and make sure they avoid offloading too much information, new ideas and suggestions.

Providing players with a constant and steady stream of information, feedback and advice can be overwhelming and often, even more so with females because they are so willing to listen and have an open mind. The very fact that female players are more willing to listen and take on board what they are being told can lead to coaches getting carried away with this. Any coach enjoys being listened to and seeing a player put things into action, but it is also easy to get carried away with this. For coaches, it is extremely important to get the right balance of delivering new information to the player while also allowing the player to work things out for themselves and allowing them to fail. Getting this balance right will mean that the player won't become overloaded with information or too over-reliant on their coach. Mistakes, errors and failing are just as much a part of the process as anything else; a player will not get better if they are being fed all of the answers.

Females are generally harsher on themselves whereas males are generally able to brush things off quicker.

Again, this is a crucial element for teachers, coaches and parents to keep in mind when working with female players. There will be no one else who is harsher on themselves than the player, so pointing out the obvious mistakes and failings is unlikely to have a positive impact. Coaches and teachers should keep their focus on how to help the player continue to move forward without dwelling too much on any negatives which might have occurred. Of course, there is absolutely a place to talk through mistakes as long as it is productive but pointing them out just for the sake of it will not have a positive impact.

Females are generally more emotionally attuned to their teammates whereas males are generally more focused on themselves.

Emotional intelligence is something most humans strive to have – to know when someone is struggling and to know how to help them is a brilliant characteristic to have. The balance of this is important and how coaches manage it can have a really positive impact on the team. Coaches don't always have insight into exactly what is going on within the group dynamic, but sometimes a really useful way to ensure team morale is high can be to set up what is often referred to as a 'players group', who help communications between the players and coaches. This will always be present at international level, but there is no reason why the concept can't be filtered down the performance pyramid. This isn't to create an 'us versus them' scenario, but rather a good way for the coach to listen to players and allow them to voice their opinions/concerns through the power of a players group, often represented by a mix of young, experienced and newer players to the team.

One aspect for coaches to be aware of, especially when you move into the performance element of the game, is the importance that players who are highly emotionally intelligent do not let this compromise their own game. Just like the advice that is given on an aeroplane, if the oxygen masks were to drop down, make sure you put your own one on first before you attend to others. This is no different in cricket; players need to make sure their own game is in order before they can start helping their teammates. Selfishness can sometimes be seen as a negative word, but there is a benefit to being selfish at times.

Females are generally more anxious and open to their challenges whereas males may have similar challenges but would be less willing to open up.

Another great attribute to have is the ability to open up about weaknesses in your game. But these shouldn't define a player. The game is yet to see any player and make them perfect, and it is inevitable that even the best players in the world will have weakness. Of course, it is important to know what they are and try to improve them, but it is not healthy to dwell on them and perhaps even compromise the time spent on developing weakness that a player forgets about their strengths or even super strengths. As with all of this, balance is vital and that is why coaches spend their careers trying to get this right.

Females' confidence generally comes from significant people (e.g., coach) whereas male confidence generally comes from within/training.

This point links into the observation of how hard female cricketers can be on themselves and with this in mind, coaches, teachers or parents must always remember how powerful it is when a player is feeling confident – much more so compared to when they are being told about their weaknesses.

Confidence translates onto the pitch and will give them more chance of performing. Obviously, if a coach was to go the other way and provide the player with too much confidence, this can lead to delusional thoughts about their ability. This in turn can be just as detrimental to that of a player who is low on confidence. With this caveat in mind, it's still preferable to veer towards providing confidence rather than not.

Help them to know how they are judged and create a psychologically safe environment for their skills to be shown.

Are they being judged on work ethic? Skill execution? Outcome? Results? Cricket is a very broad game and training will look different every week, so it is important that coaches and teachers know what players or pupils are being judged on at each session.

An example of this is when a bowler is going through a technical change; in this case, it is important to focus on the process and the progress being made with regard to the technique rather than the outcome such as where the ball is going. The focus should be on the technical development rather than the ball hitting the top of off stump. This also works the other way round, for example, a batter who is playing in a scenario at training will be told by a coach that they need six runs an over for four overs. It may be the case that the batter is scratching around, and their technique may be slightly off, but if they are achieving the outcome then they should be applauded for this rather than focus on the fact that they aren't looking technically correct.

Be consistent in your messaging and behaviours.

This can sometimes be a tough one, especially in game situations when results are on the line and when moving into performance level. It will be hard to find a coach who isn't competitive and who wants to see their team win. This is fine as long as they are consistent in their behaviours and messaging. Unpredictable behaviours and messaging can lead to players feeling on edge and not relaxed enough to focus on their game. They may constantly be thinking about what the coach is going to do or say next rather than what they themselves should be doing. Whatever style a coach or teacher has, it is important that they stick to it regardless of how their team is performing.

Back them when things don't work out.

A brilliant example of this was during the 2020 T20 World Cup in Australia when Alyssa Healy, one of the best opening batters in the world, came into the tournament in very poor form. There was talk about her form in the press and some calls for her to be dropped. Even with all of this going on, the coaching staff showed faith in her and encouraged her to continue to go out and play her usual aggressive style of cricket. This belief in her paid off in spades when she was named player of the World Cup Final having led Australia to their 5th World T20 Win.

Role clarity and role security.

This could be argued as being one of the more dominant features in female players – they like to know things in advance; they like to know what is expected of them and what role they are expected to fulfil. For coaches or teachers, knowing this allows you the opportunity to communicate with your players clearly what is expected of them, which in turn will provide a player with focus to execute their game plans.

Now on to the stars of the show, the players! Mike was asked what players can do from a psychological point of view to maximise their performances on the pitch.

Inner voice and your relationship with it – don't fight it, notice it, but do what matters

It will be hard to find a player who has had an inner voice that has been lovely the whole time. Generally, the inner voice can plant seeds of negative doubt. A simple example would be for a batter who is facing their first ball and the inner voice is telling them how good the bowler is at the other end and re-living all the times they had got out to the bowler before. The inner voice also tells the player that they didn't have a good warm-up at the start of the game, so how on earth are they going to score any runs now! As Mike has said here, it is rare for the inner voice to go away, so the best thing a player can do is to notice it is there, understand why it is there and work through how they can negotiate with it. For example, being able to notice the inner voice is telling you that you aren't in good form, then turning it around into something positive – such as 'I might not be in good form but that doesn't mean I can't score runs'. 'I will be able to find a way to score runs if I focus on the next ball and only the next ball – that is all that matters'. At this point, the player can then proceed to go through their ball-by-ball routine and focus on the next ball.

> *Strengths-based work – recognise your strengths and work out a way to maximise these in various contexts*

All too often players and coaches focus on the weaknesses of an individual. This isn't always a bad thing, especially if it is an ongoing technical point that results in a player consistently getting out. However, it is just as important to focus on super strengths for players – these are the things that players rely on for success and being crystal clear about what these are and how a player can use them will allow players to thrive and stay in a positive mindset.

> *Emotional control – finding your optimal zone*

Players often talk about getting themselves game ready. This means they know what emotional and physical state they need to be in to perform at their best – this state will vary from player to player. An example of this is to think of the optimal zone as a spectrum. At one end of it is the silent assassin and at the other end of it is the gladiator warrior. For the silent assassin to perform their role they need to be calm, measured and in control of their emotions, while the gladiator warrior needs adrenaline pumping through their veins, and they need their heart rate to be high. Former England Batter Claire Taylor used to sit on her own and listen to classical music before she went into bat – she needed to be calm and focussed, and this helped her do this. While at the other end, the gladiator warrior end of the spectrum, Katherine Brunt getting ready to bowl would need to be physically stimulated, she would need blood pumping around her body, she would need to be up and about going through her physical routines and she would need to be chatting to people – this worked for her. All players are different and knowing exactly what your optimal zone is, takes time, practice and experience but once found it can provide players with more consistency.

Routines – pre-performance, during performance

As former England women's assistant coach Jack Birkenshaw used to say, 'one day you could be batting like Donald Bradman (one of the greatest batters to have ever played in the men's game) and the next, you can be batting like Donald Duck'. Cricket is an unforgiving game, it is as unpredictable as most other sports when it comes to players' performances and their consistency. With this in mind, players need to find stability and security when they can. This often comes in the form of routines – they need something to refer back to which is deeply rooted within their game to help keep them focussed regardless of their form.

At most levels, players will have a routine they carry out in between batting or bowling balls, which gives them something to fall back on if things aren't going so well – it also helps them concentrate when they need to and stay focussed regardless of what else is going on around them.

England Cricketer Nat Sciver has a batting routine between every ball she faces which helps keep her focussed on the next ball regardless of what is happening in the game 'I have a little routine when I'm batting, I do two bat taps and, in my head, I say, "this ball"... and that helps me focus on the ball that's coming towards me'. Routines can be anything players want; other batters will adjust part of their equipment in between each ball; South African all-rounder Marizanne Kapp would undo her glove straps when she isn't on strike – things like this can help players switch off, especially when a batter is batting for a long time; they have to be able to switch on and switch off. When she is back on strike, she will tighten up her glove straps as a cue for her to now focus and concentrate. Players can play around with these until they find out what works for them.

Instructional self-talk – for example, watch the ball, or coaching yourself through a scenario in a game

This is one of the most powerful tools a player can use to help boost their confidence and belief when they are out in the middle. In a game situation, players do not have the luxury of falling back on their coach telling them what to do and effectively they become their own coach. This is why positive and instructional self-talk will help players gain focus and clarity in what they need to do. Some players have taken this to another extreme and actually written key or cue words on their forearm when batting. A specific example of this was Claire Taylor (The batter) in the 2009 T20 World Cup Final when England was wobbling on their way to chasing down a low total set by New Zealand to get their hands on the trophy for the very first time. Claire Taylor held the innings together and on the outside looked calm and unphased in doing so as she scored the winning runs. Perhaps it is no coincidence then that her only focus in her innings was to keep hitting straight, highlighted by her writing the letter 'V' on her left arm as a reminder for when she got out to the middle and in case the pressure ever got to her she had that keyword and simple coaching cue to help her through.

> Confidence building – knowing where you get your confidence from and planning your training around these. For example, a bowler doing their yorker practice.

As players develop, they will become more aware of this point. Who is the coach they work best with? Which coach gets the best out of them? Is there a teammate they speak to who fills them with confidence or gives them greater clarity on what they should do in a certain situation? Is it their parents who provide them with the belief they need to perform well?

Once a player knows where they can get their confidence from, this should provide them with the opportunity to perform more consistently. Coaches are like security blankets, and young players can work with many coaches at any one time. Another skill a player will need to master is separating the information they receive from various coaches into three categories. Think of it as arranging your email folders; a player could have three separate folders:

VIP: Information they receive from a coach which works for them and helps their game. They take it on board and apply it to their game.

Pending: Information they receive from a coach but they are not quite sure yet if they think it will improve their game or not – something they can come back to if they want.

Junk: Information from coaches which doesn't work for them which the player disregards.

Lastly, if you're a coach – don't ever get offended if on occasion your messages end up in the junk folder – remember it's about the player, not you ☺

WHAT ROLE DO PARENTS AND CARERS PLAY IN DEVELOPING MENTAL TOUGHNESS IN YOUNG FEMALE CRICKETERS?

Parents and carers have a vital role to play when it comes to developing mental toughness in female players but also in ensuring their mental well-being is in a good place. As parents, we can make both positive and negative impacts on our children, often without knowing. The purpose of this section is to provide practical advice on how we can veer towards the positive end of the impact spectrum.

Insight: Heather Knight OBE, England Captain

I saw my parents work super hard at everything they did, and I used to watch them play sport a lot as well. My mum used to play squash against a lot of men, and I used to love watching that.

American Professor Carol Dweck wrote a fantastic book called *Mindset*, in which she discusses the difference between a fixed and growth mindset. It's well worth a read if you were interested in delving deeper.

Mike Rotherham supports Professor Dweck's theories:

> *Growth mindset is critical to having a healthy relationship with high performance environments. Fixed mindsets will generally mean your relationship with performance is unhealthy. These mindsets can develop at any age and athletes can move in both directions in my experience. I don't think you are either fixed or growth. They are a continuum by which you will move up and down at various points through your life at which the context you are in will at times influence your mindset. The skill is to use your mindset to influence the context. That is the holy grail!*

Dweck's research showed that the two mindsets can be manifested in childhood. One of the key influencing factors in the research was the type of feedback a child got when they were completing a task. The types of feedback given had an impact on whether or not a child believed they could go on to complete a harder task.

To provide an example, a child who was given feedback based around their effort and how hard they were trying (You tried so hard on that task, well done) were generally more inclined to take on harder challenges because they were led to believe that experiencing success was down to their effort levels which is something they can easily control. On the other hand, those who were given feedback based on what is perceived to be their natural gifts such as 'aren't you so clever' were less inclined to take on harder challenges.

PRACTICAL EXAMPLES OF WHAT PARENTS CAN DO TO HELP DEVELOP MENTAL TOUGHNESS IN THEIR CHILDREN

Mike has highlighted two areas that he feels are important for parents and coaches to be aware of with their children/parents and we will expand on each point.

Give them opportunities to fail but ensuring that you are there consistently for them.

Parents and carers play a crucial role in the development of players, even if they aren't fully hands-on. Allowing them to fail in other areas of their life will help build the resilience and mindset they need to excel in cricket. Like a youngster playing lots of different sports, they will develop different coping mechanisms and skills which they will be able to apply when they play cricket.

Don't over protect! If you do, they never learn what their coping skills are.

'We have to prepare the child for the path, not the path for the child', Tim Elmore

This can happen a lot in youth sports, and cricket is no exception. It's not nice to see a child upset or disappointed, but it is important for their development to understand and learn that things won't always go their way. For a parent or coach to get the right balance, they need to be mindful of what situations their child or player needs to be in. For example, when players have talent, it is more than likely they will dominate at their own age group. This is great, but it is also important that they are challenged and don't get too used to always being the best player. The best way to explain it is for parents to try to avoid a constant situation where their child is the big fish in the small pond. There have been so many players who have suffered from this, and the reason is because they were never exposed to being a small fish in the big pond where they won't always be the best, where they will be constantly challenged and where they will fail. This may not sound comfortable for a parent, but in the long run, if you can drip-feed this into their journey, it will put them in a better place as they progress through the levels. It may also help a player realise what their ambitions really are – do they really want to play for England? Are they willing enough to face all the challenges that lie ahead? If they are, great; but if they aren't, that is also ok too!

The main advice here is to try to develop the player so that they can adapt to different environments rather than trying to build the environment to adapt to them. Parents are not always going to be able to control their child's environment, so the sooner you expose them to mistakes and failings, the better.

QUICK TIPS FOR PARENTS IN EVERYDAY LIFE

The car journey home

Many people will be familiar with the car journey home after training or a game. Parents only ever have the interests of their children in mind but sometimes, and often without knowing, the car journey home can have a positive or negative effect on the child's development.

All people ever want is to see their children succeed and experience good performances and results; however, the focus on these outcome-orientated thoughts should be monitored closely. See below a list of questions that can be categorised as helpful and unhelpful in the car journey home.

Helpful

- What were you working on today?

- Did you feel you improved from last week?

- Did you enjoy it?

- Did you learn anything new today?

Unhelpful

- Why did you play that shot?

- How many runs did you get?

- Did you top score?

You shouldn't have played that shot (more of a statement, but one many can't help making!)

A lot of work has been done on the amount of emphasis that should be put on results and performances at certain ages. Cricket governing bodies such as the ECB have spent time in trying to get the balance right from U-11s through to the senior level for the recommendations they provide.

It is argued that the younger ages of U-11 and U-13 should be focussed on development rather than the outcome. This means providing opportunity for everyone, letting players try different roles and sharing the game time players receive when they are playing. This is very much the opposite of how cricket was played even ten years ago, where you would have two or three outstanding players in the team who would do everything while the other eight or nine players walked away with the 'thanks for coming' title. No doubt all of the opportunity the two-thirds of players had would have helped their development, but it certainly wouldn't have helped the majority. With talented players, they are always more likely to receive lots more cricket than those who have not been identified yet.

Insight: Lisa Keightley, Former England Head Coach and Former Australian Cricketer

The best kids that I've seen come through systems are the ones whose parents are really good at just letting their kids do it without putting pressure on them. Or they know their kids are good, and they don't have to. When their child plays well or poorly, they don't really show it. They're really good at knowing when to talk to them about cricket.

ENCOURAGE PARTICIPATION IN MULTIPLE SPORTS

A question often asked is when should a child start to specialise and put all of their time into one sport? I'd suggest never, until or unless they turn professional, and it is written in their contract that they can't play another sport.

Insight: Charlotte Edwards CBE, Coach and Former England Captain

I encourage them to play multiple sports. And sometimes it's been to our detriment here. We've lost a girl to Southampton Football Club because we wanted her to play cricket and football as long as she could, but she chose the sport she liked the most and that's okay, isn't it? Football is going to benefit from a wonderful talent. So, I've encouraged them to play as many sports as possible. I was encouraged. I was allowed and it was great. I dislike it when sports say no, you can't do anything else. I think it's really good for girls. I think it helps with their athleticism, fitness and everything to play other sports.

It's important to emphasise the communication with parents. They'll work it out themselves. And I think that's a win-win situation for me, if the player actually wants to commit to cricket. Because ultimately, they've got to be comfortable with it. If they feel they're being taken away from another sport too early, they're going to resend you at some point, aren't they? Hence this football situation. We allowed her to train with both, and at 15 she decided she wanted to play football. And I was okay with that. But we tried to support her in both sports, for as long as we possibly could. And I think she could still come back to cricket if football didn't work out because she's that good. So? Again, it's all about the player, the parents, and having that collaboration between us and them.

There are numerous examples of female cricketers who have represented their country not only in cricket but in other sports as well.

Ellyse Perry – Australia (Cricket and football)

Clare Taylor (the bowler) – England (Cricket and Football)

Sophie Devine – New Zealand (Cricket and Hockey)

Suzie Bates – New Zealand (Cricket and Basketball)

Deandra Dottin – West Indies (Athletics and Cricket)

Hayley Matthews – West Indies (Athletics and Cricket)

Precious Marange – Zimbabwe (Rugby Union and Cricket)

On another level, other sports can have a direct impact on developing better skills, for example, hockey players tend to excel more at sweep shots and ramps. Basketball has helped Suzie Bates take some brilliant over-the-head boundary catches thanks to excellent spacial awareness and overhead ball skills. Deandra Dottin has run countless players out thanks to her bullet arm no doubt developed when she was learning javelin throwing as a youngster. Sophie Devine possibly has the quickest hands when striking the cricket ball thanks to playing high-level hockey, and Ellyse Perry's all-round athleticism has seen her develop into one of the best all-rounders the game has ever seen.

Lastly, playing more than one sport helps players keep a balance. As soon as a player decides to or is told to start specialising in one sport, the pressure can quickly build – putting all of your eggs in one basket can be counter-productive.

PLAYING BOYS' CRICKET

The journey of many players who excel in the game has lots of similarities ranging from playing lots of sports when they were younger to playing boys' and men's cricket. We will focus on the benefits of playing boys' and men's cricket for now. If we look at this for what it means in its simplest form, it is a way a player can overtrain so that when they play in their 'own arena' they will find it much easier than how they have usually trained. Another example of overtraining is batting against a bowling machine that is set at 90 mph when you know the quickest bowling you will ever face is 80 mph or running into a bowl on a crash mat when you know you will be running in on a nice hard surface. Playing boys' and men's cricket brings these elements of overtraining:

Facing quicker bowlers

Bowling against more powerful batters

Fielding against batters who hit the ball twice as hard

Overtraining is a technique a lot of coaches use, and it is directly linked to the term 'train hard, play easy'. Females can look at playing boys' and men's cricket in this way – a form of training that is tougher than what they will face in their own arena.

Insight: Heather Knight OBE, England Captain

I definitely recommend if a young female was comfortable playing boys' cricket. I know it's a bit different now, but the standard, I think, is still generally better if you can challenge yourself when you're younger, against boys and better players. I think that's a really good thing and it helped me a lot. It helped with my resilience as well, and I guess I had that mentality that I felt like I was always trying to prove myself because everyone was looking at me to see how I would do. Wanting to prove myself every game was a really good thing and helped me a lot in my career in dealing with setbacks and pressure.

I remember playing first-team men's cricket, and it was often really tough on difficult surfaces. You'd often see the other team putting a short leg in for you just because you're a girl and try and bang the ball in at your chest, to see how you dealt with it. That was a really good learning experience for me at that young age, probably not always a pleasant one, but one I tried to relish and tried to prove that I was good enough to be there.

HOW TO PERFORM BETTER REGARDLESS OF NERVES?

Nerves are common in all aspects of life, whether it be attending a job interview for your dream job, standing up to give a presentation in front of your peers or indeed walking out to perform on the cricket pitch. They can have varying effects on people, ranging from being so crippling that a person just cannot bring themselves to deliver that presentation or not wanting to take the field when they are playing cricket. At the other end of the spectrum, people and players can thrive on nerves; it can make them feel more alert and excited to take the field.

Nerves are caused by certain triggers within the brain because for one reason or another a person feels threatened. In its simplest form, there is a 'lighthouse' in the brain, which is constantly scanning for potential threats; it is our survival mechanism, in pre-historic times the lighthouse was scanning for threats to life. As a hunter they would pick up on a threat that could put their lives in danger, this then causes a person to go into fight or flight mode.

In today's world, the threats are very different from being hunted by a lion (for example), and in sporting terms, the threat is often simply a fear of failure; it is a series of what ifs: What if I don't perform well today? What if I get out the first ball? This the most important game of my life, what if I don't take wickets? The selectors are at the game today, this is my only chance to get noticed what if I don't show them what I can really do? It is the pressure that we (and perhaps others) put on ourselves which triggers the nerves.

In a way, compared to the pre-historic threats humans used to face, these types of threats are a walk in the park! However, everything is relative and for many sportspeople the feeling of possibly failing or not performing how they want to can be hugely challenging to cope with. With that in mind, the next part of this chapter will walk you through how you can deal better with nerves.

The people who thrive on nerves often do so because they have become well equipped (through training and experience) with coping mechanisms. As a cricketer, to develop coping mechanisms you first have to understand and recognise what physical and mental responses you have to nerves.

They can turn up in many different ways, and people experience different responses that relate to nerves, for example:

Butterflies in the stomach

Dry mouth

Sweaty palms

Increased heart rate

Loss of appetite

'Jelly' legs

Feeling of sickness

All of these are common, and many female cricketers will be able to relate to at least one of them. Learn to see nerves as a good thing. A nice mantra to think about is 'I'm not nervous, I'm excited'. Try it.

MISTAKES, FAILING AND EVEN INJURIES CAN BE GREAT!

Although they don't feel like it at the time, experiencing failure, making mistakes and even injuries can be positive things in the long term. Rarely do people make it to the top of their sport without having experienced some sort of setback, and the way in which we deal with these setbacks is crucial. For former England Cricketer, triple (yes, triple!) World Cup Winner and Multiple Ashes Winner Laura Marsh, it was actually career-threatening injuries that played the biggest part in her match-saving Ashes innings. The performance demonstrated sheer determination, focus, processes and ultimate mental toughness which all contributed to the positive outcome that the team needed.

What does Laura have to say about it?

Leading up to the innings you played, can you pinpoint previous experiences you had which enhanced your ability to show such mental toughness?

Around eight months before the innings, I underwent shoulder surgery, which was followed by a lengthy period of rehab. I was told that there was a chance I may never return to playing cricket again at the highest level. This time away from the game reinforced to me how privileged I was to play for my country and how much I really wanted to get back on the pitch again wearing the three lions.

This was definitely one of the lowest times in my career. The rehab tested me both mentally and physically. Anyone who has had to rehab a serious injury will appreciate how lonely it can be, the doubts you have about whether you will ever be good enough again, waking up every morning in pain. These things take their toll on you mentally after a while. To get through this and back doing what I loved gave me confidence and an inner resilience.

I returned to the arena stronger, more determined and more focussed. I wanted to make every opportunity count and really enjoy it. It highlighted to me that my career could end at any time and I couldn't take anything for granted. I remember thinking when I was batting, I have come through this and I am back doing what I love, I am going to make it count.

On top of these experiences, what else do you think helps build mental toughness?

There are many things that can contribute towards building mental toughness. Areas that I can identify with are:

Previous Experiences – Banking those experiences when you have been successful. Identifying what/why you were successful and building those things into your future performances. Setbacks/failures, if reviewed constructively, can also have a positive influence on future performance.

Ability to push yourself out of your comfort zone and embrace challenges – If you stay in your comfort zone, you will struggle to learn and develop.

Develop performance routines that work – In the heat of the battle, the routine will help you to focus on your job, identify what you need to do and then to execute those skills successfully and consistently under pressure.

Visualisation – This was something that I struggled to begin with, but I found a really useful tool as I got older. I would visualise standing at the end of my run-up, looking around the field, seeing the opposition batter, going through my routines and then bowling the perfect delivery.

With regard to your innings can you talk us through the process you used to cope with your nerves?

I remember walking out to bat taking some deep breaths and going through the same routine I always did on my way out to the middle – touch my toes with my bat to stretch out my hamstrings and then some quick bum kicks to get my legs going. I tried to stay focussed on my job and what I needed to do. I stuck to my processes and routines. After a little while, the nerves had gone, and I was in the battle and enjoying the challenge.

For you personally what physical and mental 'side affects' present themselves when you feel nervous?

I would feel tense and sick before going out to bat; I wouldn't sit still and would be up and about stretching and playing shots.

My heart would be pumping faster than normal.

When bowling, my grip on the ball would get a little tight and I would feel a bit rigid. Bowling some warmup balls to mid on/mid off would help to relax me.

The attitude a player has towards any sort of setback or challenge is vital. It can dictate whether they giveup never knowing what could have been, or whether they push on to improve and develop even when it's tough and even when things feel uncomfortable.

It is about being ok with failing and possibly making mistakes that might cost your team the game. The best players in the world want to be in situations where the result could go one way or the other, where they know there is a chance they could lose the game, but equally they could help their team win the game. They want to have the ball in their hand, bowling the final over of the game when the opposition needs only four to win; it is wanting to be the next batter in when they need one off the last ball; it is the attitude of wanting to step forward to give it a go when they know there is every possibility that it might not come off.

This differs hugely from the attitude at the other end of the spectrum; the players who say no when the captain asks them if they want to bowl that last over, the batter who suggests someone else to go in when they need one run to win from the last ball. These players who don't want to put themselves in these situations are also often the players who won't put themselves out of their comfort zone when they are training; they won't want to practice a new shot that they aren't very good at because they don't like the feeling of not being very good at it. They also don't like the feeling of going through the process to get better, of being a novice at something.

We have to remember that all the best players in the world were once novices, beginners and amateurs before they got to the top. They were the same as everyone else and went through exactly the same process that everyone else has to go through; they just embraced and faced challenges and setbacks by stepping forward rather than stepping backward.

This relates to what we spoke about earlier in the book about having a fixed and growth mindset, embracing the process and understanding that working hard is more important than being great at everything and not having any challenges.

CHAPTER SUMMARY

- Pay attention to the mental side of the game, not just the physical

- Resilience comes from experience and self-knowledge

- Learn to use a balance of delivering new information to the player while also allowing the player to work things out for themselves and allowing them to fail

- Learn to use the growth mindset

CHAPTER 5

Formats, Techniques and Tactics

Women's and girls' cricket faces different challenges to those of the men's and boys' games. There's a stronger likelihood of the women and girls being involved in the game for the very first time when they start playing at either a school or a club – and the age at which they start the game can always vary. With that in mind, there should be a lot of thought put into which formats to play, when to begin hardball and how the complexities of the sport should be gradually introduced into their development. This chapter outlines how it can be done most effectively.

WHICH FORMATS TO PLAY AT WHICH AGE?

The biggest challenge for a coach or a teacher is knowing which format to play and at what age. This has often been down to the expectation that's been placed on the sport over the years. Traditionally we think of cricket as a sport that's played with a hardball, wearing whites and playing a lot of overs.

With cricket changing so much now across the world, we can see that women's and girls' cricket can really start with a blank canvas. The vast majority of cricket traditions have been based around the men's and boys' games, which hasn't always been entirely inclusive throughout its history. When a young boy has been playing as a junior, they might move into year 7 and start playing with a hardball straight away – or even before that, without the option of a softball version.

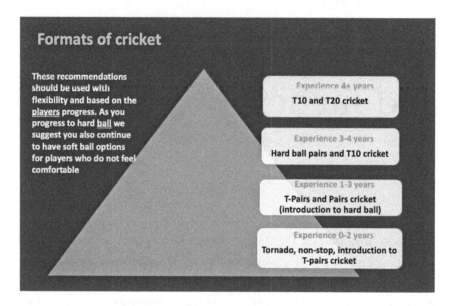

Formats of cricket

These recommendations should be used with flexibility and based on the players progress. As you progress to hard ball we suggest you also continue to have soft ball options for players who do not feel comfortable

Experience 4+ years
T10 and T20 cricket

Experience 3-4 years
Hard ball pairs and T10 cricket

Experience 1-3 years
T-Pairs and Pairs cricket (introduction to hard ball)

Experience 0-2 years
Tornado, non-stop, introduction to T-pairs cricket

As touched on in chapter 2, we advise to base things on the experience of the player over their age. If we use a scale where a young girl is either completely new to the sport or having up to two years of experience, then we'd say to play the format of the game that's non-stop and includes high levels of activity based around high levels of engagement, success and enjoyment. This may not even be an official 'format', but it's incredibly worthwhile to start with as many fun-based games as possible. It's important not to underestimate the impact a first experience has on anyone trying a new sport for the first time – if it is a positive one, they are more likely to stay in the game. At this stage, we are not trying to develop the next England player; we simply want them to develop a love for the sport. Within this zero to two years of experience threshold, you can move the players on more quickly when appropriate. A girl who has played for a year may well be ready to go up a level.

Traditionally, that's eight-a-side pairs cricket, where each pair of batters faces a certain number of overs regardless of being 'out'. Instead of giving a consequence to the batter for being out (often minus five runs), we advise to reward the bowling team instead, with five runs to their batting total. While cricket is a team sport, it's also an individual sport, and managing the accountability of players is important to ensure they won't be demoralised.

That said, there's a reasonable gap of ability needed between games-based activities and pairs cricket, so we use a bridging format called 'T-pairs'. As we now know from chapter 2, this is similar to pairs, but we include batting tees, with balls on them either side of the crease line for the batter to mark the position of a wide ball. If a bowler bowls a wide, then the batter has a free hit off one of the balls on the tees (the side the wide was bowled) – the ball that is bowled becomes redundant and the batter has three seconds to hit the 'active' ball off the tee to an area where they feel it will get them runs. **Safety point**: make sure the wicketkeeper stays behind the stumps and the batters can only hit the ball forward. This ensures there's always something for the players to engage with for every ball, and the lulls in action are minimised. When players move immediately into pairs cricket, the bowlers are still developing, and there are so many wides that are bowled that all too often the batters don't get enough opportunities to actually hit the ball. T-pairs is a nice way of keeping everyone engaged, while the bowlers still develop and the game still flows.

After developing through pairs cricket, the next level would be T-10. If you're playing a club or a school game, then T-10 gives you the opportunity to play two games in one evening. You could have an eight-a-side T-10 game where the players are being introduced to the concept of 'if you're out, you're out'. T10 is simply ten overs a side and due to its shorter nature, playing two games eases this transition as they'd still have a second chance in a later game. If you were to go straight into 20 overs or more and a batter fails early, that's the end of their evening and the end of their chances to develop batting experience. Maintaining eight-a-side also helps to keep more players fully engaged, rather than 11-a-side that has more standing around in the field – you also may not have 11 players available!

With T-10, we'd also suggest using a similar format to 'the Hundred' to minimise stoppages. This involves bowling the first five overs from one end, then the second set of five from the opposite end. This removes fielders from having to move around and changing positions between overs and slowing the game down. This can also be applied in T20 cricket by bowling ten overs from one end and ten overs from the other.

These formats should be an enjoyable and engaging transition for players who would eventually then move to traditional 11-a-side T-20 cricket. We wouldn't advise anything more than T-20 until players move into senior cricket and unless players are playing county age group cricket or have an appetite to play longer games. If there's a demand to play more than 20 overs, then that's still fine of course. We should always use this framework with flexibility, and as teachers and coaches, we should be in good positions to know when to move players and teams on.

As an overall experience guideline, we'd suggest zero to two years for fun-based activities, one to three years for T-pairs and pairs, then two to four years for T-10. Players develop at different rates, so we use a reasonably wide spectrum to cater to ability levels.

MOVING TO HARDBALL CRICKET

Within all these formats, there's also the question of when to make the transition to hardball cricket. The first point on this to make is that you have to ask yourself as a coach, a teacher or a parent whether the players *want* to make the transition. If the players are just happy to play softball cricket, then there's no rush to change this and, it may be some players never want to move away from softball cricket. In schools especially, it's important that they have the offering of both soft and hardball, and we are increasingly seeing schools and clubs take this approach. A great example is Trent College in Nottingham where both soft and hardball cricket is offered to every year group throughout the school – it seems to be a trend being set and followed by many other schools and clubs to ensure players and pupils don't drop out.

We have a process that we follow to make the change as smoothly and enjoyably as possible. The first thing to say is to not just throw them straight into a hardball game or net session straight away. At this stage, they wouldn't even have had a chance to get used to wearing the equipment. While they're still using softballs, you can just let them have a go at trying on all of the gear so they can get used to the feel of it. We've all seen the straight-leg running, where the kids forget their knees bend! We use games and competitions for who can get padded up the quickest or relay races to help show them how it feels, how it should be worn and how you can move well in it.

The image below demonstrates a step-by-step process you can follow to help make the transition to hardball cricket as smooth as possible for players.

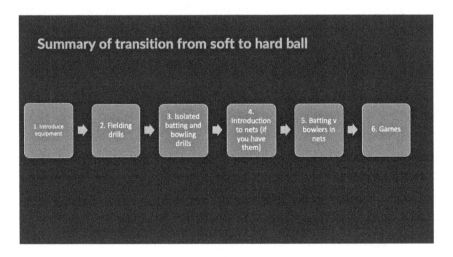

Depending on how much time you have per session, you could deliver these six steps within either three sessions (more than 60 minutes per session including two steps in each) or six sessions (less than 60 minutes per session – one step per session).

Step 1: Introduce the Equipment

Already identified is the fact that wearing equipment such as pads, gloves and a helmet can feel rather alien for first-timers. Before we even consider letting the players hit some hard balls, we should first help them feel more comfortable in the kit. Lay out all of the equipment and chat them through how it should be worn. Follow this up with some fun relay races where teams have to pad up, sprint to a mark and sprint back before unpadding for the next one to go. The familiarity they will feel when it comes to playing the game in the equipment should not be underestimated in terms of the impact it will have on their confidence levels.

Step 2: Fielding Drills

Once they have the feel of the equipment for batting, we recommend the next step to focus on introducing the hardball through fielding drills. This usually begins with isolated fielding drills. This can be as simple as getting them into pairs and have them underarm throw and catch together. This can progress to some underarm rolls, so their partner is attacking the ball, picking up and underarm throwing back to their partner. Coaches need to remember that the weight of the hardball means their release point for throwing (underarm and overarm) will be different from throwing (or indeed, bowling) a softball. We need to allow them to work this out for themselves while they're not under too much pressure. You can then start to hit some catches at them, gradually progressing to higher and higher catches as they get more comfortable – at this point, we would expect them to have developed a safe and efficient catching technique.

Step 3: Isolated batting and bowling drills

Batting

The last thing we want to be doing is sending a batter who has never faced a hardball before to the end of a net to face a bowler who has never bowled with a hardball before. There are a lot of variables within this that could go wrong. Just as the fielders will need to work out a new release point for their overarm throw, the bowlers will have to do exactly the same when bowling with a hardball for the first time. A release point for a player coming from softball bowling is likely to be quite early, and if this is kept the same for bowling with a hardball the batter is likely to be facing a beamer as their first experience batting in a hardball net – hopefully, we can all agree this wouldn't be a good first experience!

Isolated batting drills: If you're lucky enough to have access to nets, we would recommend splitting your group into smaller groups so that you can have two groups working in each net as long as it is safe. You can set up a circuit of different batting shots to allow the players to get used to hitting the hardball for the first time with a wooden bat. Again, it is important we allow the players to get used to batting with a wooden bat compared to a softball bat – the biggest difference will be how much heavier the wooden bat will be, then pair that with a heavier and hardball it will take some time for players to get used to. Below is an example of the drills you can set in the circuit:

1. Front-foot drive (using a bobble feed – this is an underarm feed that bounces a couple of times before it gets to the batter)
2. A pull shot (with an underarm feed 'on the full' – this is a feed that doesn't bounce before it gets to the batter. The aim of this feed is to replicate the delivery for which a pull shot will be played to)
3. Use of feet
4. Challenges: You can be creative on this station. As an example, with your players padded up, they can each have a ball and their first aim is to hit the ball up and down on the bat as many times as they can before they lose control. Think the footballing version of 'keepy uppies'. Within this challenge, their aim is to try and get the ball to bounce on 'the middle' of the bat every time. 'The middle' of the bat is the part of the bat where if the ball is struck in the middle, it will often go further than if it hits any other part of the

batter. People often refer to it as the sweet spot, and as a general rule it is often in the lower half of the bat.

Bowling

For players bowling with a hardball for the first time, you can simply set the stumps out, perhaps with a target and simply let them run in and bowl. The aim will be for the players to get used to their new release point and build up their confidence with no thought of worrying about the batter at the other end.

All of these drills are designed to isolate the skills, so you're not adding in any variables. If you put them straight into having a bowler bowling to a batter, there are far more variables. The bowler won't be sure where the ball is going, and neither will the batter who has never faced a bowler with a hardball before.

This stage is also a good time to introduce the concept of net safety.

After you've introduced them to the individual skills, you can now move on to step 4.

Step 4 and Step 5 – Introduction to the Nets

If you haven't already done so, your first port of call in these next two steps is to go through the net safety (step 4) with your players. Once you have done this, they are ready to go and practice in the nets. Depending on how many nets you have access to and using the guidelines of no more than eight players in a net, you can have two players batting in a pair who rotate every four balls they face. You can have two players padding up as the next pair to bat while the remaining four players will take turns bowling.

If you have too many players for eight in a net, then you can split the whole group into two, so while group 1 is training in the nets, you can have group 2 set up doing something else, for example, fielding or practicing their bowling. The groups can then swap halfway through the session or if you are tight on time the groups can swap the following week.

PADDING UP AND NET SAFETY

INTRODUCE FUN RELAY GAMES AND RACES TO HELP THE PLAYERS GET USED TO
PUTTING ON AND RUNNING IN THE EQUIPMENT

PADS

- KNEE ROLL ON THE KNEE
- STRAP ENDS ON THE OUTSIDE
- TOP STRAP SLIGHTLY LOOSER

GLOVE

- THUMB PROTECTOR SHOULD BE ON BOTTOM HAND

THIGH PAD

- GOES ON THE THIGH OF THE FRONT LEG

HELMET

- SHOULDN'T MOVE OR SHAKE ABOUT WHEN RUNNING

RUNNING A NET

- NO MORE THAN 8 PLAYERS PER NET
- 2 BATTERS: 6 BOWLERS OR 1 BATTER: 7 BOWLERS
- TIMED BATTING SLOTS
- ALLOCATE ORDER BEFOREHAND

NEVER TURN YOUR BACK TO THE NET

ALWAYS WATCH WHAT IS HAPPENING

NEVER PICK A BALL OUT F THE NET HEAD FIRST

BATTERS SHOULD ARM ARM ROLL OR UNDER ARM THROW THE BALL BACK TO
THE BOWLER

NEVER BOWL THE BALL IF THE BATTER ISN'T LOOKING

NETS CAN ALSO BE USED TO PRACTICE DRILLS...

Step 6 – Game Ready!

Your players are now ready to go into hardball games and training.

WHEN SHOULD PLAYERS START TO SPECIALISE IN A PARTICULAR SKILL?

This is a difficult question to answer in any precise way. The most crucial element to this is that at that introductory level, players should be encouraged to have a go at all elements of the game. Don't just see this as batting/bowling/fielding/wicketkeeping. All elements should include off spin, leg spin, seam bowling, quicker bowling, attacking batting, defensive batting, close catching, boundary catching and so on. Every player should be encouraged to try every single skill.

Insight: Charlotte Edwards CBE, Coach and Former England Captain

Try and be an all-rounder for as long as you can because it's a much more enjoyable game, isn't it? Again, I think it's a conversation. They start to work out which one they're better at and which one they have the most passion for. And I think that's the skill of the coach, to actually keep having those conversations with the player. And they'll know when it gets too much. There's generally a time when they realise that they're better at one than the other, and they enjoy training at that one thing as well.

As they progress through the levels and eventually get to the T-10 and T-20 levels, that's often the time they'd start to think about specialising in certain elements of the game. It should also be remembered that aside from wicketkeepers, fielding is the one element that they all should be working on constantly throughout their development (and beyond!).

TACTICS

Tactical considerations are something that can be gradually introduced to players as they progress through the physical skills of the game. In pairs cricket, we'd suggest giving the players quite a standard field. The image of the standard field will provide bowlers with protection on both the leg side and off side while having fielders in positions to stop the batters from taking singles too easily.

Pairs field setting & A side

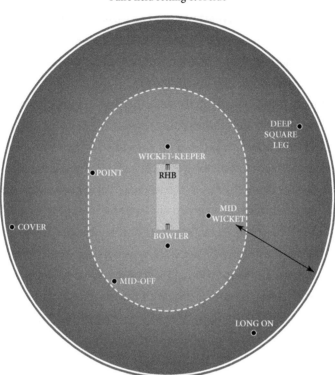

Assuming batter is leg side dominant

At the pairs level, it's about introducing the concept of what the fielder's role is. As a general rule, if they're close to the bat (in the inner ring, as we'd call it for more advanced groups), it's for them to understand that their role is to stop the singles and prevent the ball from going past them. If they're on the boundary, their job is to stop the ball going over the boundary, but also to stop singles turning into two runs as well.

At this level, you might start talking about field position names. You can do this through some games in training or during game warm-ups. We use a game where we call out a field position (marked out by cones) and have the players run to that position – you can introduce a consequence for the last person or two to make it if you want to be competitive about it!

When they get to the T-10 stage, that's where we'd say to start teaching them about setting fields and discussing the benefits it has on the game.

There's a lot to think about, particularly if you're a captain or a bowler, and it's worth teaching players the basics relatively early in their development. We encourage all players to think like a captain, even if they're neither captain nor a bowler. They should always be encouraged to think 'what would I do in this situation?'

With that in mind, learning to set a field is an important thing to consider. They should be thinking about what the batter's strengths are. This can often be shown by picking up cues as to where they like to hit. If they have quite an open stance (where you can clearly see the toes of their back foot), they're likely strong on the leg side; conversely, a closed stance (you can't see their back foot or you can see the heel of their back foot – see pic) suggests a mindset to hit through the off side. These strengths can then be seen as signs of possible weaknesses. That closed stance should encourage bowlers to bowl as straight as possible as the batter might struggle to hit the straight ball if they're closed off. Field settings should be adjusted according to this, with a more off-side dominant field for the closed stance, while laying traps for the straight ball on the leg side.

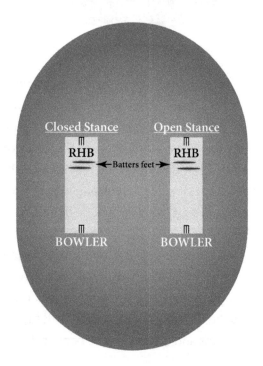

Setting the field should also look at what insurance the bowler would like to have. If the bowler has a 'bad ball', then they'll need some cover for it, should it happen. If they're prone (as many are!) to bowl the leg side half-tracker (a ball that bounces halfway down the pitch), then the captain and bowler should think about giving them some protection out on that leg-side boundary. The mindset can sometimes be that having fielders out on the boundary is a negative/ defensive move, but it can actually be seen as a positive, wicket-taking move. If you have a deep square leg and a deep mid-wicket fielder, then you're saving three runs every time, not to mention the opportunity for catches in the deep. It's about seeing field setting as a positive influence on the game and every fielder making a positive contribution.

One other point to consider when setting a field is the situation of the game. When a batting team is chasing down a total, the number of runs they have left to chase can also dictate the fields a captain and bowler choose to set. For example, as a fielding captain, if you have a lot of runs to play with, then you can afford to have lots of fielders on the boundary to prevent them from scoring boundaries and fielders in the ring can 'sit on it', that is, they don't have to be in really tight – when you have lots of runs to play with the threat is not the batting team taking singles – it will be to find the boundary often. On the flip side, if as a fielding team, you don't have many runs to play with, then you will have to consider having more fielders in the inner ring to stop the easy singles to try and create pressure and therefore create a mistake from the batting team – this is a balancing act because by bringing fielders in to stop the single you are also running the risk of allowing batters easier chances to score boundaries. This is when you might revert to having one fielder on the boundary either side for the protection while everyone else is stopping the single. These situations will also highlight the importance for the bowlers as well as the captain to be clear on what they are trying to achieve.

A few notes for the images:

The attacking fields are generally used when a new batter comes to the crease, as they are often at their most vulnerable. The attacking nature of the field settings can also restrict the batters from scoring freely.

The defensive fields are used when a batter is either 'in' or the situation of the game means you need to restrict the boundaries. They can also be used when a bowler might be struggling to bowl the ball where they would like.

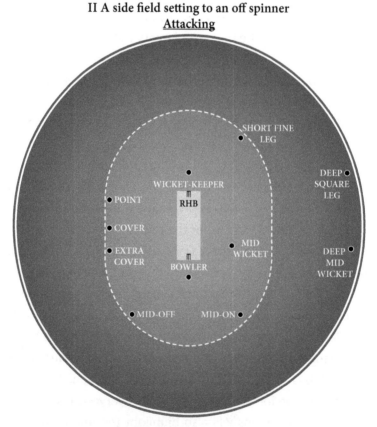

II A side field setting to an off spinner
Attacking

With an off spinner - as a general rule
we can assume the batter will try and hit
with the spin ie to the leg side

If you wanted to be even more attacking as an off spinner, you could take the short fine leg out and put them into slip as a wicket taking option.

II A side field setting to an off spinner

Defensive

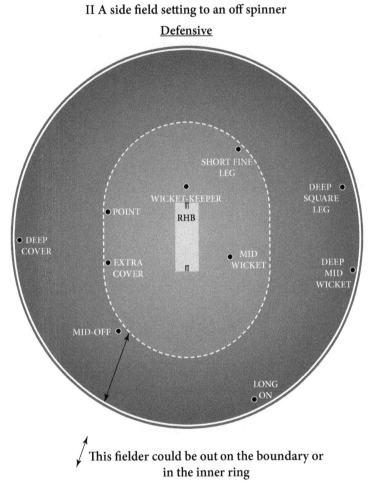

This fielder could be out on the boundary or in the inner ring

Assuming you have to have five fielders in the inner ring, you can alternate between having a deep cover or long off out depending on the batter's strength and where the bowler is looking to bowl.

II A side field for a leg spinner
(Attacking)

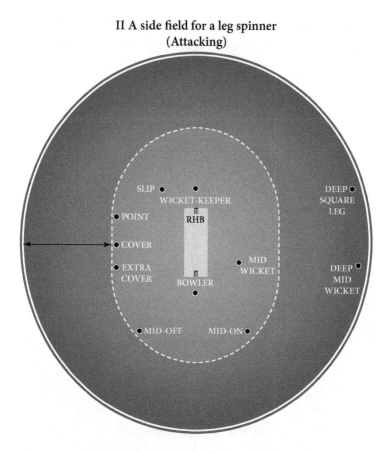

Leg spin is arguably the toughest bowling style to execute consistently, so it is important that the captain gives them the best field setting possible to allow them to feel confident and in control. Starting with deep cover out is also an option and will provide the leg spinner with protection at the start of their bowling spell while still having an attacking option of starting with a slip.

II A side defensive fielding setting for a leg spinner
We can assume the batter will hit with the spin
hence why we have got 5 fielder on the offside

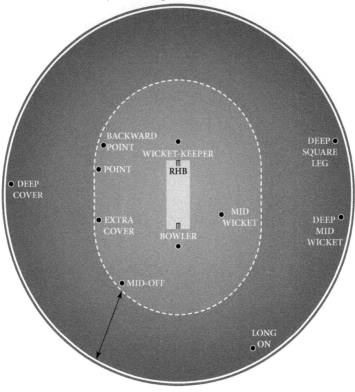

This fielder could be out on the boundary or
in the inner ring

Depending on the batter's strength and where the bowler is trying to bowl, there is also the option of moving backward point to short fine leg. This would be especially relevant if the bowler is trying to bowl straighter or if the batter likes to play the paddle. Similar to the off spinner, you can also alternate between having deep cover and long off – if the bowler is trying to bowl a straight or leg stump line, then you can afford to have cover up and long off back as an example.

II A side field setting for an inswing bowler
Attacking

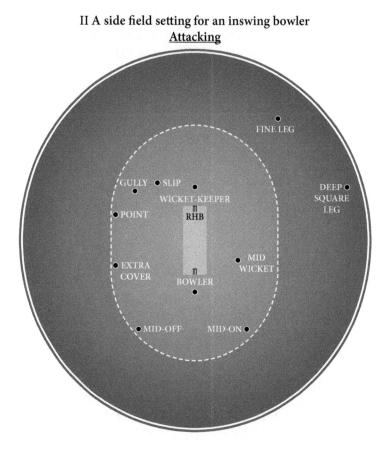

For inswing bowlers, one of the first ways they are trying to get a batter out is either bowled or LBW. If there is a lot of movement through the air then leaving cover vacant will tempt the batter into trying to drive through the off side which can bring bowled into play as well as caught behind. If the batter gets a few through the covers then slip can be taken out to plug the gap and gully could be sent down to third.

II A side field setting for an inswing bowler
Defensive

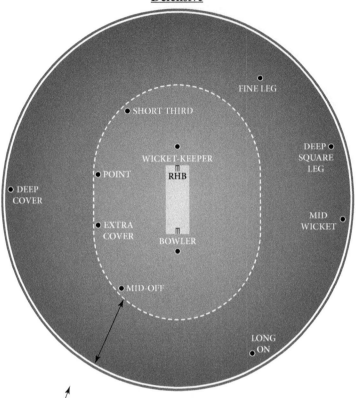

If the bowler is looking to bowl straighter
you can bring deep cover up into the ring and
put mid off back on to the boundary

II A side field setting for an outswing bowler
<u>Attacking</u>

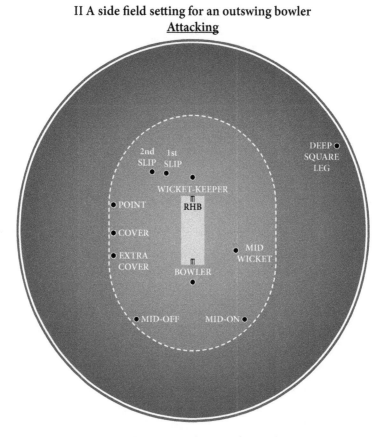

If you wanted to be super attacking, similar to the inswing bowler, you could leave cover vacant and put them in behind the bat as another catcher.

II A side field setting for an outswing bowler
<u>Defensive</u>

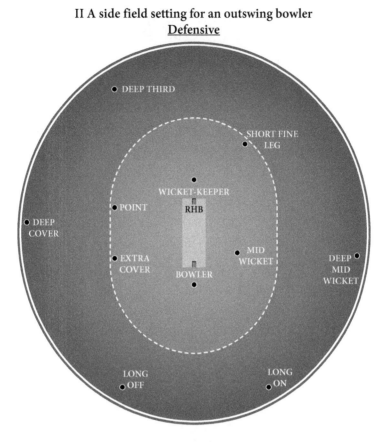

It's then worth discussing which player is most suited to each individual fielding position. The normal rule for younger players is to put the best fielders in the positions where the ball will be hit the most. While this is reasonably self-explanatory, it's well worth the captain and bowler taking it into consideration.

CONCLUSION

We'd all agree that the most important element of any sport is the fostering of enjoyment at the early stages. By introducing women and girls to cricket with the right formats and the right developmental path, we can ensure they have the opportunity to enjoy the sport from the very beginning. This in turn will lead to greater participation and increased benefits for all those playing, no matter their experience levels.

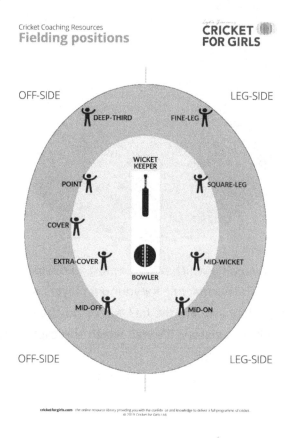

Cricket Coaching Resources
Fielding positions

CRICKET FOR GIRLS

OFF-SIDE   LEG-SIDE

DEEP-THIRD   FINE-LEG

WICKET KEEPER

POINT   SQUARE-LEG

COVER

EXTRA-COVER   MID-WICKET

BOWLER

MID-OFF   MID-ON

OFF-SIDE   LEG-SIDE

CHAPTER SUMMARY

- Learn which format is right to play, for each individual player
- Concentrate on enjoyment and engagement
- Make the switch from soft ball to hard ball as smooth as possible
- Gradually introduce tactical knowledge alongside batting/bowling/fielding

CHAPTER 6

Practical Games, Drills and Coaching Tips

One of the biggest challenges for any teacher or coach is being able to develop and increase the basic skill levels of the players in a fun and engaging way. Often, and especially when working with younger ages new to the game, their attention span is shorter, and their desire to spend purposeful time honing and repeating certain techniques is minimal. That is why when we are introducing the basics of cricket, we need to do so in a way that is engaging and fun while also providing opportunity to get better at the basics of cricket.

In this chapter, we will provide you with simple games and drills that provide a fun way for your players to develop the basics of the game. Referring back to chapter 5 where we went through the pyramid of what format to play and when, these games will be ideal for getting anyone up and running with players new to the game with zero to two years of experience.

Before we get into the nuts and bolts of this chapter, the following is a bit of a checklist of the main outcomes we want to help our players achieve when introducing the game:

Basic bowling outcomes:

- Bowl with a straight arm
- Understand how they can bowl with a run-up

- Have an action that is repeatable and safe from injury
- Ball bounces once before it arrives at the target
- Understand where they should be positioned on the crease

Batting outcomes:

- Knows where and how to stand at the crease (side on and with one foot on either side of the crease line)
- Has a backswing and understands why it is important
- Has a desire to hit the ball hard
- Hands are close together on the bat

Fielding outcome:

- Can throw overarm and underarm
- Can attack and pick up a moving ball with one and two hands
- Understands the basic technique for catching and throwing
- Understands what position they need to be in before the bat is about to hit the ball

WHICH BALL TO USE AND WHEN

Sponge/Foam Balls: Perfect for beginners as well as young players. Also, it is the best option when playing in enclosed spaces such as a small sports/assembly hall. If ever you are worried about the safety of your players due to an enclosed space and/or windows, this will be the safest option.

Tennis Balls: The perfect ball when introducing cricket. Also, it is the best option when introducing batting drills. Using tennis balls doesn't mean you're not playing 'proper' cricket, so don't be afraid to use these even when working with better players. International players use tennis drills as part of their training diet on a regular basis.

Incrediballs/Wind Balls: The best ball to use in-between soft and hardball cricket. The incrediball has the features of a cricket ball such as a stitched seam, while the wind balls are often the bright orange many of you would have seen before. The wind balls are generally bouncier and work well on Astro turf and grass, while the incrediballs also work well on these surfaces as well as indoors. Both are great options.

Cricket Ball: There are two weights of cricket balls for females to use. They are based on age:

- 4 and ¾ ounces for U-13
- 5 ounce for 13yrs+

GAMES TO DEVELOP BATTING AND FIELDING

With all of these games, we recommend that a tennis ball is used and that the coach or teacher is the bowler to keep the game flowing and ensure the batters receive balls that are hittable. If you have confidence in the player's ability to be accurate with their underarm bowling or if you would like to give them the chance to develop it, then that would be okay as well, just be mindful of the quality of delivery the batter is receiving.

If you have larger groups and if space allows, you can split the group into four teams to have two games going on at a time. If you have the time, you could even get a mini World Cup going!

The 3T Challenge

This is the best game to start with to help hone the basic principles of batting, such as the 'step and swing' motion used when playing the front-foot drive as well as the basic setup. It also introduces the concept of trying to hit the gaps as a batter and avoid the fielders. Lastly, it introduces the competitive element of the team that has the most runs as wins. If a batter is halfway through completing a run then it will not count. *Batters cannot be out in this game.*

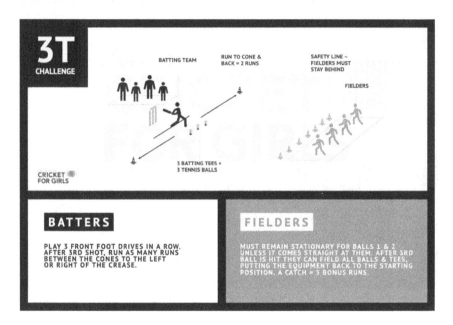

Tornado Cricket

This is great because it reinforces teamwork and gets lots of players engaged. The fielding team will realise that the most effective way for them to play it is by at least six fielders being busy – three players collecting a ball, plus three players standing next to each 'T' ready to receive the ball from one of their teammates to place it on the 'T'. There will also be a wicketkeeper ready in case the batter misses the ball. There is also no reason why you can't have more than three balls in play. Tennis balls are the best and safest balls to use for this game.

From a batting point of view, they get three chances in a row to hit the ball giving them a higher chance of experiencing success in one go.

If a player is halfway through completing a run, then the run will not count. *Batters cannot be out in this game.*

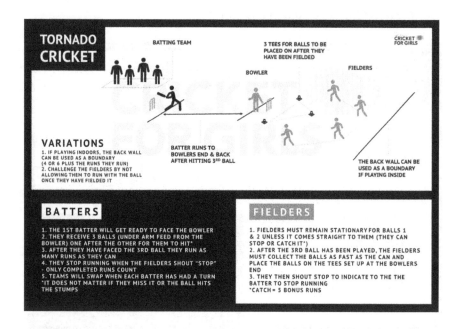

TORNADO CRICKET

CRICKET FOR GIRLS

BATTING TEAM

3 TEES FOR BALLS TO BE PLACED ON AFTER THEY HAVE BEEN FIELDED

FIELDERS

BOWLER

VARIATIONS

1. IF PLAYING INDOORS, THE BACK WALL CAN BE USED AS A BOUNDARY (4 OR 6 PLUS THE RUNS THEY RUN)
2. CHALLENGE THE FIELDERS BY NOT ALLOWING THEM TO RUN WITH THE BALL ONCE THEY HAVE FIELDED IT

BATTER RUNS TO BOWLERS END & BACK AFTER HITTING 3RD BALL

THE BACK WALL CAN BE USED AS A BOUNDARY IF PLAYING INSIDE

BATTERS

1. THE 1ST BATTER WILL GET READY TO FACE THE BOWLER
2. THEY RECEIVE 3 BALLS (UNDER ARM FEED FROM THE BOWLER) ONE AFTER THE OTHER FOR THEM TO HIT*
3. AFTER THEY HAVE FACED THE 3RD BALL THEY RUN AS MANY RUNS AS THEY CAN
4. THEY STOP RUNNING WHEN THE FIELDERS SHOUT "STOP" - ONLY COMPLETED RUNS COUNT
5. TEAMS WILL SWAP WHEN EACH BATTER HAS HAD A TURN *IT DOES NOT MATTER IF THEY MISS IT OR THE BALL HITS THE STUMPS

FIELDERS

1. FIELDERS MUST REMAIN STATIONARY FOR BALLS 1 & 2 UNLESS IT COMES STRAIGHT TO THEM (THEY CAN STOP OR CATCH IT*)
2. AFTER THE 3RD BALL HAS BEEN PLAYED, THE FIELDERS MUST COLLECT THE BALLS AS FAST AS THE CAN AND PLACE THE BALLS ON THE TEES SET UP AT THE BOWLERS END
3. THEY THEN SHOUT STOP TO INDICATE TO THE THE BATTER TO STOP RUNNING *CATCH = 5 BONUS RUNS

Non-Stop Cricket

This game will introduce the concept of being out. While in 3T Cricket and Tornado Cricket, there is no consequence for being out, Non-Stop Cricket introduces this concept to facilitate player's understanding of the game. Rather than the player being out and not getting a chance to play any further part in batting, the batting side simply loses one of their physical bats which represent a 'life', a bit like a computer game, once the batting side loses all of their 'lives' the teams swap over.

If you are working with less experienced players, then you can increase the number of physical bats as the batting team starts with an anticipation that they are likely to lose their lives more frequently.

Similarly, if you are working with more experienced players then you may want to give them fewer physical bats to start with as it is likely it will be harder to get them out. *Ways of being out in this game include bowled, caught and hit wicket (where the batter hits their stumps as they try to hit the ball).*

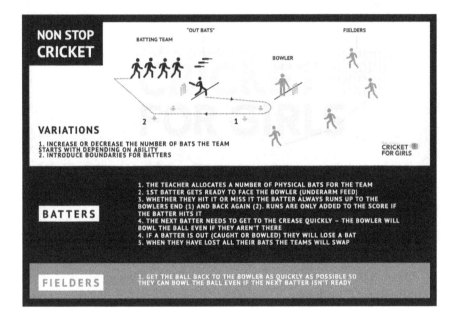

Pavilion Cricket

This is a great way to introduce the concept of run out to both fielders and batters. As well as being out bowled, caught and hit wicket, in this game batters can be run out at the bowler's end. Once the batter has completed the run at the bowler's end, they will walk back to the end of their team's batting line. The maximum a batter can score from one ball is a safely completed run plus any boundary scored. An underarm bowl is suggested initially to help players understand the game quickly, once this has been achieved, you can introduce overarm bowling by the fielding team. Two to three deliveries per bowler will help keep the game flowing and ensure the maximum number of players are involved as opposed to each bowler bowling a six-ball over.

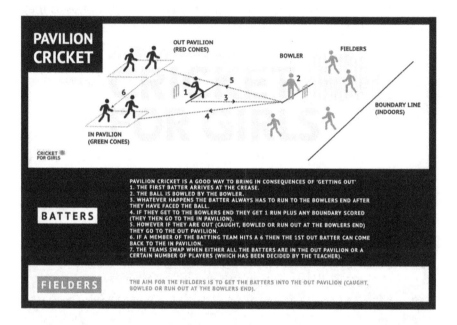

Caterpillar Cricket

The perfect game to defy the notion that cricket involves too much standing around, and also perfect for a chilly day! Caterpillar cricket keeps everyone active and is a great game to develop player's fielding skills and teamwork – it is also a good warm-up even for the more experienced players. If you are playing the game inside, then it is suggested for the number of players who have to complete the fielding challenge is higher compared to if you are playing outside where we would suggest a lower number of players completing the fielding challenge. The reason for this is because the fielders will be able to get to the ball more quickly inside compared to when the ball has been hit outside which is likely to involve a long run for fielders to get there!

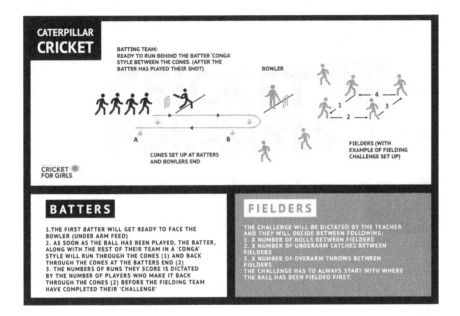

CATERPILLAR
CRICKET

BATTING TEAM:
READY TO RUN BEHIND THE BATTER 'CONGA'
STYLE BETWEEN THE CONES. (AFTER THE
BATTER HAS PLAYED THEIR SHOT)

BOWLER

A   B

CONES SET UP AT BATTERS
AND BOWLERS END

FIELDERS (WITH
EXAMPLE OF FIELDING
CHALLENGE SET UP)

CRICKET
FOR GIRLS

BATTERS

1. THE FIRST BATTER WILL GET READY TO FACE THE
BOWLER (UNDER ARM FEED)
2. AS SOON AS THE BALL HAS BEEN PLAYED, THE BATTER,
ALONG WITH THE REST OF THEIR TEAM IN A 'CONGA'
STYLE WILL RUN THROUGH THE CONES (1) AND BACK
THROUGH THE CONES AT THE BATTERS END (2)
3. THE NUMBERS OF RUNS THEY SCORE IS DICTATED
BY THE NUMBER OF PLAYERS WHO MAKE IT BACK
THROUGH THE CONES (2) BEFORE THE FIELDING TEAM
HAVE COMPLETED THEIR 'CHALLENGE'

FIELDERS

THE CHALLENGE WILL BE DICTATED BY THE TEACHER
AND THEY WILL DECIDE BETWEEN FOLLOWING:
1. X NUMBER OF ROLLS BETWEEN FIELDERS
2. X NUMBER OF UNDERARM CATCHES BETWEEN
FIELDERS
3. X NUMBER OF OVERARM THROWS BETWEEN
FIELDERS
THE CHALLENGE HAS TO ALWAYS START WITH WHERE
THE BALL HAS BEEN FIELDED FIRST.

BOWLING GAMES

As with all skills in cricket (or any skill for that matter!), players need time and repetition to develop the fundamentals. As alluded to earlier on in the chapter, how we choose to do this is crucial in ensuring players stay engaged with the game. The following games are recommended to be used with an element of competition to provide players with focus and motivation.

Box Bowling

A simple game that puts focus on where the players are looking for the ball to bounce before it reaches their target. The ideal length of delivery from a bowler is when the ball pitches in an area where the batter doesn't feel they can get on their front foot and play a full-blooded drive, and also where they don't feel they can get on to the back foot to play a scoring shot such as the pull or cut shot; if the bowler gets the length right then the batter invariably has no other option but to play a forward defence. In terms of the line of the ball, in simple terms, a ball that is hitting the stumps is a big tick. The size of the box can be made larger or smaller depending on the ability of the players you are working with.

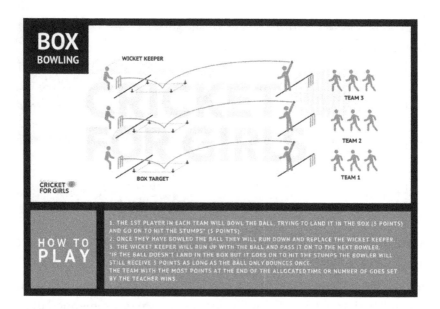

Scatter Cones

This is a fun way to introduce a more enhanced focus on where the players are aiming to pitch the ball before it arrives at their target. Scatter the cones in an area that compliments the focus on where you would like your players to pitch the ball.

Bullseye Bowling

The quest to bowl the perfect delivery! Bullseye bowling is the toughest out of the three bowling games purely because the target is the smallest. A great one though for the players who simply won't stop until they have hit the target!

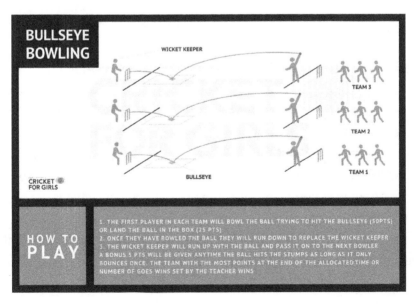

For all of these bowling games, it is worth mentioning a couple of points about how you set them up if you are making it a competition. Most players really enjoy competition, but in their haste of trying to complete the skill quickly, it can sometimes lead to a poor technique.

You have two options for how to run the competition:

1. **Timed:** For example, you might set up four stations of the scatter cones game and split the group into four teams. You will then set a time (three to four minutes) for the teams to start and get as many points as they can in the time allocated. This creates drama, but it can lead to players rushing and not bowling properly.

2. **Number of goes per player**: The setup with be the same as above, but instead of setting a time, you can allocate a number of goes per player, for example, three goes each. This means they are not under time constraints and are more likely to execute the technique with more attention.

Lastly, we recommend that either tennis balls or incrediballs/wind balls are used for these bowling games.

THE CRICKET FOR GIRLS FIELDING FRAMEWORK

Fielding is often a part of the game that isn't given enough time – the importance of it is very often underestimated, and we can forget how many game-changing moments have happened because of one piece of fielding, as well as the fact that it is the part of the game players have to participate in 50% of the time! As coaches and teachers, there are many different things we can do to develop our player's fielding, but it is important we understand what the priorities are and what is the best way of improving our players.

At Cricket for Girls, we have put together a fielding framework that we are confident will help coaches and teachers understand where the focus should be when players are introduced to the game and as they progress.

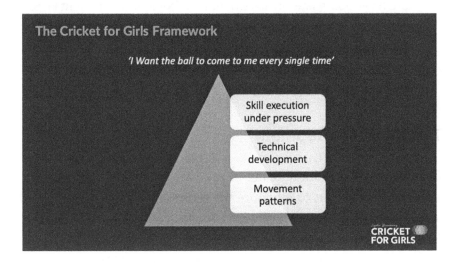

How Does It Work?

The fielding framework aims to provide teachers and coaches with a guide of what is important when introducing fielding.

Starting at the bottom of the pyramid, the most important aspect of developing good fielders is **movement patterns**. If players can't move efficiently and with good footwork, then their chances of getting to the ball to take a catch or enforce a run out are smaller. So, before we start thinking about putting all of our attention on catching and throwing techniques, we should first help our players move more efficiently.

How Can We Develop Movement Patterns?

1. Encourage your players to get involved in other sports
2. Ladder work and movement patterns using cones (this can be included in your warmups or set up as a circuit)
3. Small-sided games such as 'hand hockey'
4. Ensure drills are completed with maximum intensity

5. Reinforce a good body position when moving
6. Instruct players on how to move effectively; for example, if you are developing lateral movement then being low with bent knees and short sharp steps is most effective
7. Provide players with time to find out what their best 'set position' is. The set position is the position they should get into as the player is about to hit the ball.

Technical Development

Once we have introduced some of the basic elements of movement patterns, we can start to introduce the technical element of fielding. A really good way to develop technique is to allocate ten minutes of practice for a certain skill at the start or end of each session. Regular technical work will help the brain remember the movement which will in turn make it become a more natural and programmed movement. Below are a few focus areas for basic fielding skills such as catching and throwing:

Catching:

- Head close to the ball
- Whole body movement
- Strong hands
- Eyes and head still before taking the catch

Throwing:

- Big Base
- Front foot pointing at the target
- Head going towards the target
- Throwing arm above shoulder height
- Engage front shoulder and non-throwing arm

Once the basic technique has been covered, you can then start to integrate both movement patterns and fielding techniques into your drills. For example, if your players are working on their lateral movement from one cone to the other, why not add in a catch every time they arrive at a cone, you can then even challenge them to throw the ball at the stumps once they have taken the catch.

Execution of Skills Under Pressure

Once players have grasped the main movement patterns and technical skills, we can then challenge by asking them to execute the skills in pressured situations. Training under pressure will help identify technical weaknesses and strengths which means you can then spend more time working on certain skills accordingly.

Ways to create pressure in training:

- Competition (teams, 2v2, winner stays on, etc.)
- Timed challenges (complete as many catches as you can within two minutes)
- Consequences (losing team has to complete a challenge set by the other team)
- Match situations
- Develop fatigue (it is harder to execute skills when players are physically fatigued)

Fielding Mindset

Underpinning all of the above has to be that the players want the ball to come to them. A positive mindset when fielding is one of the most powerful tools we can equip our players with. We want to make fielding a fun part of the game that players can't wait to get involved in.

One final way to help your players be one step ahead:

We have spoken a lot about practical skills in fielding, and this is always the best place to start. However, there are other ways we can help our players excel in the field. One of these ways is by helping them understand what anticipation is and how they can use it to their advantage in a game. See below a few things to get them thinking about:

1. **Look at the shape of the batter**: The way the batter is shaping up can often give fielders clues as to which direction the ball is going to be hit. For example, if the batter has gone on to their back foot with a high back lift, it is likely they will be playing an attacking back foot shot such as the cut shot; in this instance, the point fielder should have picked up it is coming their way. Another example is if the fielder sees the batter using their feet to advance down the pitch, this indicates they will be playing a front-foot shot making it likely that mid-on and mid-off will be in the action.

2. **Put yourself in the batter's shoes**: This is a great way for the fielders to engage with the game and anticipate what might happen. For example, if the batter is new to the crease, they will be keen to get off strike as soon as they can. This means fielders may need to be ready to stop the quick single.

3. **What is the situation of the game?** Does the batting team need 10+ runs an over? If so, it is likely the batters will be searching for a boundary, this will often mean (certainly at the recreational level) a legside shot, so the fielder at the deep mid-wicket or deep square leg should be ready!

4. **What is your role?** Captains put fielders in positions for a reason. To keep it as simple as possible, if a fielder is in the inner ring then their job is to stop the quick singles and also to stop anything going past them to prevent boundaries. However, if you are on the boundary your job is to stop two runs being taken and also to stop the boundaries.

All of these points will help fielders be one step ahead of the game and give them the best chance of having a positive impact on the game.

How does it work?

- Players need a foundation and a method
- The underpinning factor determining good fielding is how a player moves (*movement patterns*)
- Many players can execute the basic skills (*technical development*) such as catching, throwing and stopping; but they aren't able to execute the most basic movement patterns.
- Similar to a batter in their set up, or a bowler in their run up, inconsistency and inefficiency isn't conducive to helping players execute skills consistently , and when under pressure (*executing skills under pressure*). *Highlights poor technique*
- The one component aligned to all three levels is the players mind set which has to be, "I want the ball to come to me every single ball".

CRICKET
FOR GIRLS

CHAPTER SUMMARY

- Use the combination of introducing and enhancing cricket skills with fun and engagement
- Don't forget to spend enough time on fielding drills
- Encourage players to be involved with other sports
- When players have grasped basic movement skills, ask them to perform them in pressure situations

CHAPTER 7

Selecting and Using the Right Kit

Cricket equipment and clothing for females are a part of the game which have been overlooked for many years. For such a long time, females have had to 'make do' with oversized and ill-fitting clothing, as well as equipment which just doesn't give female players the best chance of succeeding. The good news is that this is gradually changing, and some brands now see and understand the benefits of ensuring they are offering something that is suitable and helpful for female players.

We are often asked why females need different equipment and what impact does it have? In this chapter, we will address the key differences in equipment and clothing for females along with helping to provide some useful tips on what equipment people should be looking to buy when they are starting their journey in the game.

Why do females need equipment and clothing specific to them? This isn't about 'pinking it and shrinking it'; it is about acknowledging the genuine reasons why females will benefit from more tailored equipment and clothing no matter how small the changes might seem to some.

The most obvious place to start is to highlight the fact that the body shapes of females and males are completely different, and because of this 'unisex' approach, men's sizing just doesn't cut it.

PADS AND GLOVES

Traditionally pads and gloves have been sold based on sizes for men and boys. Up until now, brands have never considered the differences in hand/wrist sizes for gloves and leg sizes for pads. The straps on female-specific gloves and pads are shorter, which means players won't have the 'overhang' of straps when wearing them.

Not only do these changes provide better fitting equipment, but the overhang of straps also has a direct impact on performance. For example, it has not been uncommon for batters to be given out caught behind due to the umpire mistaking the noise of the ball clipping the overhanging strap for the ball skimming the edge of the bat down the legside.

BATS

From the weight of the bat being offered to the design and colouring/branding on the bat, we all have different tastes which is why it is so important players are offered something that is more likely to be suited to them. Providing more lightweight cricket bat options for female players is crucial. A bat that is heavy can hinder performance by reducing bat speed through the ball and limiting technical ability. The design of the bats can also be more suited to female tastes, not all females will want pink bats, some will and some won't, so ensuring there is something for everyone is also important.

CLOTHING

This is a big one. For far too long, females have had to make do with ill-fitting clothing which just isn't flattering or comfortable. Many female players will be familiar with the crotches in their trousers being down by their knees, or the short sleeves of their playing shirt feeling more like a three-quarter-length-sleeve. Female body shapes are different – very different! Feeling comfortable in clothing can breed confidence, and confidence can have a direct impact on performance levels on the pitch.

Clothing also isn't just about being the right fit. It is about what colour teams/clubs/schools decide to play in. Some people find it an uncomfortable point to address, but the fact of the matter is that females have the reality of dealing with periods every month. For a young girl or indeed adult female taking up cricket for the first time being handed a pair of cricket whites to play in could instantly put them off even considering taking up the game. I have had many conversations with females who came very close to not continuing with the game because of the stress and anxiety that came with praying they would not 'leak' in the three hours they spent fielding. This is a very real worry and a potential barrier to participation in a wonderful sport.

A couple of points to help overcome this being a reason for females not to take the game up:

1. Move away from tradition. Does the team really need to play in cricket whites? If the answer is no then why not consider the option of a dark pair of playing trousers like black or blue?
2. If the team does have to play in cricket whites then there are some brilliant period-wear brands that provide underwear that prevent any sort of leaking. Check out The Female Cricket Store (see more details later in this chapter) which offers a variety of colours. The period wear can be worn with or without tampons; they are that good.

LABELLING

The labelling of cricket equipment and clothing is a bugbear for many females involved in the game. It alienates females from ball one (!), but it is such an easy thing to change. Men's, small men's, boys, small boys, adults, juniors and youths – we don't think this is too much of a change for brands to make, and we are really pleased to say that many brands have already made these changes which is great. For the female-specific equipment: women, youths and girls, while 8, 10, 12 and 14 for the clothing. The change of labelling by brands is incredibly important and welcome, not to mention overdue.

Although some of these points may seem minimal or insignificant to some, for the majority of females playing the game it makes a huge difference, from making them feel more included and welcome to the game of cricket to having and seeing the tangible benefits out on the pitch.

If you are based in the United Kingdom, you can visit The Female Cricket Store (www.thefemalecricketstore.com) that offers equipment focussing solely on female cricketers of all ages and abilities, soft and hardball players.

> The Female Cricket Store provides equipment specifically suited for female cricketers and those working with female cricketers in schools, clubs and counties. All products are hand-picked by a team of female cricket specialists who understand what is needed during each step of your cricketing journey from beginners to advanced and for all ages.
>
> *www.thefemalecricketstore.com*

EQUIPMENT

What do you need?

Whether you are new to the game of cricket or a seasoned pro, there are some musts when it comes to buying your equipment.

Essentials	Optional
Cricket Bat	Thigh Guard
Helmet	Abdo Guard
Pads	Arm Guard
Gloves	Chest Guard
	'Inners' are a lightweight and thin pair of gloves that can be worn under your batting gloves

BUYING YOUR FIRST BAT

Size

The image below shows you what size is recommended depending on how tall you are. For female adults and taller youths, the short handle would be the most appropriate size. This provides players with more control over the blade compared to the long handle. Harrow is a bat size smaller than the short handle and is often suited to slightly shorter female adults. Some brands also offer a 'small adult' sized bat.

Player Height	Bat Size
4' to 4'3" (up to 130cm)	1
4'3" to 4'6" (130cm to 137cm)	2
4'6" to 4'9' (137cm to 145cm)	3
4'9" to 5' (145cm to 152cm)	4
5' to 5'3" (152cm-160cm)	5
5'3" to 5'5" (160cm-165cm)	6
5'5" to 5'7" (165cm-170cm)	Harrow
5'7" to 5'9" (170cm-175cm)	Small Adult
5'9" + (175cm+)	Short Handle

Weight of the Bat

One of the most common mistakes cricketers make when buying a cricket bat is that it is too heavy.

As long as you have got the right size bat, then the lighter it is the better.

This allows you to have more control over your shots and also helps you generate quicker hand speed.

When buying a short-handle bat, the lightest weight available from most brands is 2lb 7oz, so unless you know you prefer heavier bats, we would advise opting for 2lb 7oz. If you are looking at smaller sizes then you rarely get the option of picking a weight, for sizes between one and harrow, it is best to pick a bat based on your height.

Type of Willow

Willow is the type of wood used to make cricket bats, and there are two types to choose from:

English Willow: The best one. Grown in England and has the highest quality wood. The growing conditions in England mean there is more moisture in the wood, resulting in the cricket bat lasting longer and giving a better performance. This type of cricket bat is the preferred option for those playing and training on a regular basis from school or club level upwards. As you would expect though, with better quality comes increased costs; however, it is likely that the bat will last for longer.

Kashmir Willow: Grown in India in the dryer and hotter conditions mean the wood is dryer, harder and a little denser which often results in heavier bats. However, cricket bats made of Kashmir willow are brilliant for those new to the game and playing recreationally – all at a more affordable cost. So if you are unsure of how often you will be playing or if you are just dipping your toe in cricket, then Kashmir Willow bat will be a good option for you.

Grade of the Willow

Willow is graded by number, with Grade 1 being the best (and most expensive) to Grade 5 being the least expensive. The grade relates to the appearance of the bat. For example, Grade 1 will be free from any marks or blemishes as well as having straight grains (the lines you can see on the face of the bat). The further down you go through the grades, the more you will see markings and discolouring to the bat. It is worth pointing out that the grade of the bat should not affect the quality of the wood.

See below for how to pick your grade depending on what level you play:

Grade 1: Top club standard and above

Grade 2: School and club level

Grade 3: School, social or lower-level club standard

Grades 4 and 5: Beginner

Your Budget

We understand cricket is an expensive sport to play, and we hope that the above guide provides you with the information you need to buy a bat that is relevant to your needs and suits your budget. Some brands offer equipment bundles which can work out cheaper if you are buying everything in one go.

Knocking Your Bat In

Most bats these days arrive in a pre-knocked-in condition. This is where the bats have been knocked in via a machine, making them ready to use as soon as you receive your bat.

However, we would recommend additional knocking in just to make sure your bat is ready to use.

Below is a step-by-step guide to knocking in (if your bat arrives with an anti-scuff sheet on the front then you do not need to apply linseed oil and can go straight to knocking in the bat).

Apply raw linseed oil to the face and edges of the bat evenly, two to three teaspoons of oil is the correct amount. Rub into the face of the bat and its edges. Do not oil the back, labels or the splice of the bat* (*where the handle fits into the blade). Do not over-oil the bat, as this will deaden the fibres of the timber and affect performance. Leave the bat horizontal and face up to **dry for 24 hours.**

If you are planning to **use the bat in its natural state**, that is, without an anti-scuff sheet, then **repeat steps 1 and 2 twice** more. If you are planning to have a protective anti-scuff sheet fitted then one initial coat of oil is sufficient.

Wipe off any excess oil and **knock your bat in with a bat mallet for approximately 4 hours.** (If you do not have a mallet to knock your bat in, then a long sock with a cricket ball inside will work just as well!) The edges and toe of the blade require particular attention using glancing blows off the face to harden and round these areas. Care and attention should be made not to hit the edges, toe or back of the bat directly as this will cause damage. The knocking in should be performed with gradual increasing force, but never too hard to cause damage.

Fibre tape is applied to the edges of the bat and an anti-scuff sheet is fitted over the top if required.

Test the blade using a good quality old ball during a light net session or having 'throw downs'. If seam marks and indentations occur, further knocking in is required. Go out and enjoy your new bat!

With the increased visibility of the women's game on TV and in the press, young females can now see people that look like them. There's a duty for clubs, schools and brands to now help these young players emulate by being able to wear gender-appropriate clothing and use gender-appropriate equipment. With all of these small (and big) wins, we move closer to equality, and we make huge strides towards growth.

CHAPTER SUMMARY

- Females need benefit greatly from specific clothing and equipment designed for them

- Ensure the equipment you use is the right size and weight for the individual player

CHAPTER 8

Equality, Diversity and Inclusion

Equality, diversity and inclusion (EDI) is a subject that has long been at the forefront of cricket and sport more generally. Sometimes this is for positive reasons; sometimes this is for entirely negative reasons. Cricket has seen all too much of the negative in both recent times and in years gone by. If we want the game to be inclusive for *everyone*, then we need to work together in order to make this happen.

Rather than write a chapter myself, based entirely from my own experience which will be very different to so many other people's experiences, I wanted to bring into the book the perspective of some of those working at the forefront of EDI. I wanted to showcase the work that is going into it, to ask for advice on how best we can bring about positive change and to help educate us all on the different challenges faced by those who mightn't have the access to cricket that can be taken for granted.

We're incredibly lucky to have contributions from Ebony Rainford-Brent and Chevy Green on the *ACE* programme, from Shruti Saujani on the *Dream Big Desi Women* initiative, from Jodie Hawkins of the Sydney Sixers who've done so much in the LGBTQ community and from Ian Martin, discussing disability cricket.

I hope we can all learn from them and be inspired by the work they've done and continue to do. It's so important to the game and to the people it should be including and representing.

EBONY RAINFORD-BRENT AND CHEVY GREEN, ACE CHAIR AND DIRECTOR OF PROGRAMMES

ACE stands for the African-Caribbean Engagement programme. This was set up due to the 75% decline in black professional players in the past 25 years. These numbers aren't great and have been going backwards for some time. It's been worrying to see such less number of black players breaking through to the county game, which then filters up to the international level.

We set ACE up with the ambition to find the best talent that exists out there and try to make sure there's support for those players to break through. We also want to help at the grassroots level and try to develop much younger players. We also do outreach work to working-class areas, no matter the ethnic background as those in lower socioeconomic areas can face the same problems with access to cricket. This might be facilities or cost of equipment or any number of things. The aim is to give back to these communities and provide opportunities for those within them to have better access to the game.

There's an awful lot of talent across many different sports that come from these communities, so why not cricket? At the moment, there's a class issue with cricket where a lot of elite players come from private education and not enough from more diverse communities in both the boys' and girls' games. Whether they go on to become professional players, club players, coaches or administrators, we want to empower more people to enjoy the game that we've loved for so long.

It's going to take some time, but we're hopeful that we can tackle the challenge.

We have a three-pronged outreach strategy. We have the academy for the more talented players who might be close to achieving county trials. We then have our community hubs to connect those in the communities to the game. Finally, we have our schools programme. This involves going to schools to offer cricket to primary years 4, 5 and 6 as well as a targeted year 7 and 8 programme, predominantly for girls.

For clubs to encourage female players from African-Caribbean backgrounds, we'd encourage them to be proactive. Do as much outreach into diverse communities and schools as you can. Some clubs might not have huge amounts of diversity, which may be partly down to location. You've then got the flipside where people from those communities see a club and may think it doesn't necessarily represent them.

If you're the 'only' person at a club, it can be quite hard, but if as a club, you end up attracting a cluster of three or four kids, you'll notice that everyone just feels a bit more comfortable being part of a club. The more outreach work that's done, the more chance you'll have of attracting multiple new players from different backgrounds which have a knock-on effect of attracting more on top of this.

It's then about clubs being considerate of different cultural things that can impact people. It might be a case of learning more about a certain culture, which can be hard to do but could also be fun to do. Clubs can celebrate black history month or international women's day. Continuously celebrating lots of different events can really help to drive positive perception of your club and help to attract players. It shows the culture of your club is based around caring for all sorts of groups, whether it be ethnic diversity, disability, gender diversity and others. This goes for schools as much as it goes for clubs. Young people nowadays are more aware of issues around things like diversity or climate change and other broader societal challenges that weren't case just a few years ago. If your club or school doesn't show a positive side to this, then the young people know this, and it has an effect on their enthusiasm to become involved. It's important for clubs that want to be progressive and want to keep young members coming through, that you understand what's going on with young people.

To do this, schools and clubs should work hard to build the right team of people to help drive all of this forward. By the 'right' people, we mean those who can be welcoming, who can communicate well with a wide range of people and who have enthusiasm for what they're trying to achieve. Just one parent, coach, volunteer or teacher could bring 30 new kids to the game just by being the right person.

SHRUTI SAUJANI – SENIOR MANAGER FOR CITIES AND VOLUNTEERS AT THE ENGLAND AND WALES CRICKET BOARD

The Dream Big Desi Women program was set up to inspire 2,000 South Asian women into volunteering roles through our national programmes. We know that statistically speaking, South Asian women are less likely to volunteer and less likely to be active, so making it an easy entry point through Dream Big was a good starting point. We know that South Asian women are more likely to get involved in an activity if it's related to family or culture, and we know the South Asian community loves cricket as well. Bringing cricket national programmes with the family together was a great opportunity. It's all about creating role models to inspire the next generation but also to create opportunities for young children to start from ages 5 to 11 to enjoy their first experience in cricket and have a great time.

There's a lack of South Asian role models of women like them or girls like them who are involved in cricket. We know when you see a friend or you see someone that you aspire to be like, you're much more likely to do it. Families sometimes don't advocate being involved in sport, because they don't see it as a viable and sustainable career option. I think the timing of when cricket training takes place is often not at the right time that fits around family or cultural events that happen. We know South

Asian families have big families and include a lot of big events. There's a year-round celebration of events and festivities and often sport takes a backseat because it tends to fall in that time. I don't think the sport has been taken to these communities. There's always been an expectation that women will walk through the door, they'll come to us, we've got an offering. What's been different through Dream Big is that we've taken cricket to the community in places where they feel safe and where it's comfortable for them.

So what can clubs actually do?

One of the most significant influences of the ECB is the imagery that all potential players, coaches and volunteers will see. When I started three years ago, the imagery would usually be a white male. But then you're trying to target South Asian girls, and this just doesn't work. Using appropriate poster images with girls of different backgrounds definitely significantly increases the likelihood of attracting players from these communities.

Using appropriate language is also incredibly important. The game is beginning to move from batsman to batter, which is welcome, but not the end point by any means. I'd suggest keeping language simple and broad and for clubs to really think about *all of* the different communities you're trying to serve, so everyone feels welcome.

It's also important to think about when the children and families do come, they're made to feel welcomed rather than simply siloed into the environment that's already been created. Make sure that you have someone who is a welcoming host for new families or you have someone who will help with the logistics of signing up. One of the challenges I've seen is that South Asian families might be less savvy with technology and find the online registrations more difficult. At our club we've arranged for drop-in sessions, where families can come along and we'll help them sign up on the day. We've put a lot of emphasis on aligning flexibility and support. We have flexible payment options and make sure that we can still accept cash payments. It's really about creating as many small wins as possible to make it straightforward for families from all backgrounds to get involved.

My personal experience playing cricket and going to clubs is being the only Asian girl going into a club and looking around, with no one there that looked like me. We've looked at ways of improving this and one of the changes we've made is modest apparel or culturally appropriate kit. If you look at a sports kit, it tends to be fitted, so one of the things we've done through Dream Big is to make it more culturally appropriate. The introduction of hijabs, also loose t-shirts, not skin-tight and loose jogging buttons. Also, we give the women and girls a choice of what they'd like to wear rather than just giving them kits. Giving people choices and options is always a positive thing and removes as many barriers as possible to their enjoyment and engagement in the game.

Further advice I'd give as well is to have a space where people can share feedback. So having a really clear feedback loop, letting people express if there's anything that doesn't work and creating safe spaces where people can air their concerns or even give positive. That's how Dream Big has been built.

Dream Big came from the women themselves, it was something they wanted and that we executed from an NGB perspective. It's been built by the women for the women, which is awesome.

I wanted to finish with some success stories, to show the impact the programme and more like it can, and do, make.

We've had huge success in community settings. As an example, we've had Mosques where the Imam has helped to champion women playing cricket. We've seen the same support in Temples. We've seen community partners who've helped to advise clubs on creating culturally appropriate environments. They've helped ensure there are changing rooms, fitting rooms and toilets: all the little things that are in place for women and girls to come to take part in cricket.

We've seen a lot of good case studies of women who've stepped up and overcome huge challenges. We've seen several volunteers who have secured full-time jobs, many of whom would never have thought about the possibility of a career in cricket prior to Dream Big.

We've helped women overcome mental health difficulties where in one example, becoming an activator was one woman's outlet for being safe and being comfortable.

In 2019, we trained over one hundred volunteers to become mental affairs aiders; little did we know the pandemic was going to hit. And we know that mental health can be a taboo subject in the South Asian community. These hundred women have been champions throughout the pandemic to support these women through what was a really difficult time. We know South Asians were one of the groups that were more significantly affected by COVID. These women became a community and volunteered to give back more and that all started with Dream Big. It's been a huge mixture of elevating women in the South Asian community, getting full-time jobs for some of them, improving their mental health, but also celebrating some great stories as well. One story that stands out is about a lady in Manchester who'd never worn western clothing. We gave her the activator kit, and she'd hide it every time her family used to visit, but her son would always bring it out and announce 'my mom's a cricket coach'. That actually changed her family's perception and culture of what sports can do for someone.

I'd encourage every coach, club and school to look more into what Dream Big is. At the heart of it is the philosophy that the more people we can encourage to play cricket, the greater our game gets.

JODIE HAWKINS – SPORTS ADMINISTRATOR

We've done a lot of work towards building women within the game and attracting more women to the sport.

We decided that doing community work in the LGBT-plus community was going to be really critical to our success, both practically and commercially. Anyone who tells you they're doing community work without a commercial lens is probably lying, and we were really upfront with Proud to Play, who was the partner that we worked with, and they were the same.

But it's also the right thing to do.

And I guess for me personally, having had friends who've come out and been uncomfortable in that, I hated seeing it. I wanted to create an environment, especially in the men's game. I think it's quite well known in the women's game that we have both hetero and homosexual players. But in men's team sport especially, it's largely unheard of. I knew we had a group of players that would be really receptive to creating that inclusive environment; we'd always had a culture of being really family-focussed and treating everyone like they were a member of your family. It just seemed like a really natural fit.

That got us started, and we were then introduced to Ryan Storr from Proud to Play and everything developed from there. I get frustrated when people talk about women being a diverse group of people; we're actually 51% of the population in Australia, so that's cute. And we had already done that work there, so what else do we want to do? And the natural fit for us seemed to be the LGBT-plus community.

For the most part, our work has been really well received. I have a feeling that everyone's probably sick of hearing from me, but there's a need to be relentless. I don't like anyone who slaps a rainbow flag on something, pats themselves on the back and says job well done. That's not enough. I think sport has a responsibility to drive change and *real* change.

We understood the importance of driving that change through the grassroots as well as the elite levels. With Ryan, we worked on developing education programs for clubs and predominantly entry-level clubs rather than grade clubs.

We started working with a group called rainbow families, which are families of same-sex parents. And the beautiful thing that you find out once you start working with communities like rainbow families is that the parents of kids in those rainbow families, when the kid finds a sport where they feel included, those parents are twice as likely to volunteer for the club. There's this really lovely thing about feeling like they are included.

We worked on very specific markets, looking just to be in the west to start off with where there is a very strong LGBT-plus community in that area. We were quite strategic about it. But we also had a social media strategy, because goodness knows the second you say something on social media someone will argue the counterpoint. We were really clear from the beginning that we've always been about education, not ranting and yelling back at people. So, part of being inclusive means that you also need to understand that other people do have opinions. Being inclusive means you need to listen and respect their desire to have an opinion. But that doesn't mean that we have to agree with it, and hate speech obviously has consequences. So, we worked really hard on what our responses would be in that social media space.

We were really clear about making sure we had some good messaging to go back with. Over the years those negative comments have sort of dropped off a little bit, albeit they're still out there. I realise, of course, you get the 'oh, when is heterosexual day'. It's like, are we really having this conversation? But I would take the time to go and respond to them. So we were really respectful of people's opinions but then ask people to respect the reason why we were doing things. We try to take the soft approach, the educational approach, as opposed to no, you're wrong. Let's take every opportunity to educate someone or at least have them open their minds a little and ask questions. And that over the years has really evolved in the way that we do respond to people and I think has been a really positive influence on the community.

There have inevitably been some barriers to what we do. There are sections of society where they push back. Some people just don't want to acknowledge that the LGBT community exists. They don't or that's not a lifestyle that is acceptable to them. There's always this uncomfortable part that I think people are just challenged by. But there's also the old sport and politics don't mix which drives me mad because what does a politician do if they want to get a vote? They'll go and lobby at a sports event with a mate, pint of beer and a shirt. And it makes them look like the everyday Australian. So, that whole sport and politics don't mix. I mean, we just sat through the Paralympic Games, and Todd Hodgetts, one of the intellectually impaired athletes who competed, did a shout-out to Scott Morrison. And what did Scott Morrison do the next day? Made sure he got a video call with Todd Hodgetts that went onto the channel 7 news. That's just a lie, a flat-out lie that sport and politics don't mix.

Sport is effectively a religion in Australia. Using it for positive change is really important.

The 'sport and politics don't mix' group is usually the people who are uncomfortable with the conversation. But I would say the trend is, especially with the younger generation improving quickly. While there are people who push back, I think they're becoming less and less prominent.

So what can clubs do to ensure more inclusivity?

You don't necessarily need an additional headcount for it. It shouldn't be someone's job; it should be the way that you go about your business. And the best thing I can always suggest is that people go and educate themselves, and I know there are resources in the UK just as there are resources here, where you can go and get that education on how to create that inclusive environment. A lot of it just comes from understanding the emotional driving force behind the community that you want to engage with.

You shouldn't need someone who's going to sit there and go, well, we're going to put this sticker on the door to make sure people know that we're an inclusive environment. The thing we discussed a lot about community cricket is that we didn't want to create bespoke LGBT competitions. It wasn't about that. It was about using our existing footprint and just inviting more people into it. So, gender-neutral bathrooms, simple things like that, once you're aware of them, it's actually not a great additional workload. It's just about changes in language; it's about some slight changes in facilities. I mean, at the SCG, we just turned the disabled bathrooms into gender-neutral bathrooms. So, once you're aware of the things that make people feel included, it's actually not that big a job to do it. And it just became part of our everyday. We have a fan engagement specialist at the Sixers, but his job wasn't inclusion; his job was to engage fans and inclusion just fell into that. But if the events manager doesn't think with a mindset of inclusion then our events don't look the way that they need to look. And if our sponsorship team doesn't consider inclusion and our digital and media team doesn't consider inclusion, then again, you're not going to have the right filter on everything that you're doing. So it's less about dedicating a resource and more, I think, about educating yourself about the things that make your environment inclusive and just implementing them.

You still need someone to champion it, absolutely. You need someone who's prepared to at least set the plans in place, get people thinking about it and ask the right questions. But every Cricket Association, to be fair most sports associations across the world, is run by middle-aged white men. And it's just about having someone who can champion it and ask the right questions. Again, a bit of education. So, why are we doing this? Being able to build. If it's a participation case, a business case or whatever it is that is going to get that leader interested in what you're trying to do. The Sixers, it just so happened that I was in charge so I was like, let's just run at it and go for it. But not every organisation is going to have that. So, it's just about understanding what your club wants. Everyone's looking for participants, everyone's looking for volunteers. What understanding **what** engaging a diverse market and creating an inclusive environment can do to tick those boxes will often get people interested. And just asking the right questions.

It's hard, because it's really about balancing; we talk about balancing for profits. So in major sports, you're there to make money because the only way you can keep growing your business, growing the grassroots and doing all the things that you need to do is by driving revenue. So, you have to balance your for-profit with your for-purpose. And if you can get the two to meet in the middle like we did with the LGBT community and understand the value of the pink dollar in our area and what it could mean for match days and all those sorts of things. That's often the way in the door with people who don't necessarily think that inclusion is an important pillar strategically to have within your business. So, drive it back to the pillar that they think is important: driving cash, driving revenue. And that can often be the way in.

Thinking about the situations in other countries, inclusion comes in many, many forms, and many countries are going to be behind. Afghanistan has now gone back to Taliban rule where women's rights are so much less. Inclusion might look different anywhere that you go. But you have to start somewhere. Australia, probably 15 years ago, started considering more females in executive roles. And once you open the door to inclusion, other sorts of things can start to come in: whether it be ethnic or religious inclusion, sexual inclusion, all those sorts of things. As long as you're opening the door to a conversation around inclusion, I think that's the really important piece to start off with. I couldn't tell you the number of times that I've presented to delegates at cricket New South Wales and they literally come up to me and say, I have no idea what you've just talked about, but it all sounds great. Some just won't ever understand it, but if they can see the sport growing off the back of it, it often kills off any of the questions they might have.

Subconscious Bias

It's interesting because subconscious bias gets thrown around now like it's always a bad thing. But I know when I walk down the street, if it's at night, and I'm on my own, and I see a group of men, my immediate reaction is that those men might be the most harmless people on the planet, but my subconscious bias is saying, get over the other side of the road, get past them, they're gonna hurt you.

Subconscious bias is built-in sometimes for a reason. The way that you start to engage people in changing those biases is by asking questions. I'd be asking what are the generic questions you can ask where you know people are going to go to a certain answer that highlights the subconscious bias that everyone has. And then what are the questions that you can loop back to that would start to open their mind around some of the other inclusion issues. A lot of people might say we don't treat women any differently than men. And I think, well, I've been called aggressive all my entire life. And if I was a male, it would be assertive. I can't even begin to explain how frustrated that makes me. Just because I have an opinion and I'm an assertive person with confidence doesn't mean I'm being aggressive. I'm not yelling at you. I'm not trying to slap you with the information I'm giving. But that is a bog-standard, subconscious bias that happens. Until you start raising it and making people aware of it in a non-confrontational way because no one ever wants to feel that they're being racist. No one ever wants to feel that they're being sexist.

But what are the questions you can ask that get people thinking? Why is that not necessarily right? That's when you start to open your minds a little bit. For probably 18 months we discussed doing unconscious bias training with CEOs. And the CEO would often say 'no, no, it's a waste of time'. No. Because when you talk about subconscious bias or unconscious bias like that, people feel that you're telling them what they can and can't think. And that's not really true.

What we're trying to do is open their minds a little bit to different ways of thinking. It's why diversity is so important in management and on boards and all those sorts of things because it opens more doors than letting everyone think the same thing. So, I would be posing it as a series of questions. What are those questions that make you realise that you do have that unconscious bias that you apply to everyday life? And then what are the ones that you would ask around inclusion that may get people just thinking a little bit more about oh, actually, I probably do that. It's about training yourself to catch it in the moment of thinking of it and then thinking, oh, actually, that's what you're projecting onto that person, or into that situation. You need to step back and ask yourself the question, what could you do better? What could you learn? How could you be more inclusive? And why it isn't about me, it's about the person at the receiving end of it? It's the way you ask the questions and get them thinking as opposed to telling people you need to think this way that's going to change some of those biases.

If you can be open to learning and to developing and evolving, that's the bit I think is super important. Just the understanding that you'll probably learn as you go, we all do, and that you'll never reach perfection, because my personal opinion is perfection never exists. But if each day you just try to do things a little bit better, and learn from experiences, that's the most important part. What communities need and want will evolve over time as well. So, what we're doing now might look like rudimentary stuff in another five or six years' time. But it's the steps; we've got to use the steps to get there. You look at how long it took for women to get the vote, full-time employment and all these other things. It's not about immediate change. We should be speeding up change because it should never take as long as it has in the past. But it's about learning every day and just continuing to improve. But you need people who are open to thinking about it and being questioned on it and understanding that it's not about challenging my personal belief system. It's about making sure we're creating a safe space for as many people who want to be involved as possible.

IAN MARTIN – HEAD OF DISABILITY CRICKET (ECB)

We run national squads for those with physical disability, learning disability as well as blind and deaf players.

The mistake that some people can make is that it all gets lumped together and is simply called 'disability cricket'. Within physical disability alone, there are hundreds of different types of disabilities. Our aim is to provide a playing offer that's appropriate for everybody within the context of their unique situation at a level that works for them.

We have table cricket for those with a high level of support need. It's still recognisable as cricket but simply played in a different way to meet the needs of that group. We then have games of cricket that most watching from the sidelines wouldn't even think was played by those with a disability, then with all the levels that come in between, it's a huge scope to cover.

Clubs or schools that have disabled players expressing interest in joining have various options. First of all, it would depend on the level of disability of the player. As an example, if they had a prosthetic limb they may be perfectly capable of playing and training in a usual way, or providing whatever assistance is needed based on their requirements. A player may also turn up in a motorised wheelchair where playing a mainstream game might not be appropriate for them. It may be possible to adapt a coaching session to enable that individual to participate insofar as practical.

We currently have a partnership with the Lord's Taverners, who deliver the 'super-1s programme'. This is taking place in 22 counties at present, with the aim of growing to 38 counties. This involves taking the game to places where disabled people are, including day centres and special schools. Rather than expecting individuals from those environments to leave a space where they feel safest, we can bring the game to them. If there are then players from those environments showing either a talent or an enthusiasm to join a mainstream club, then we can help with that as well.

The first thing a club needs to do is talk to the individual as to what their needs are. Then it's possible to have an honest conversation about how the club could possibly support. Even if there were practical things in place such as wheelchair access, it still needs clubs to have the right attitude from the club members and administrators to help facilitate. This is very similar to women's and girls' cricket. If the club isn't open to it and enthusiastic towards it, it won't work for the player.

Clubs and counties are recognising more now that the game has to be accessible to all, and it's our aim to maintain and build on this momentum.

County cricket boards are a good place to start for clubs to access more information and potential funding. The CPAs (County Partnership Agreements) are very significant in this. The ECB essentially formed a contract with the county cricket boards to say that if you're going to continue to receive funding, they have to deliver on elements including disability cricket.

The other thing we have going at the moment is a scheme called 'Champion Clubs'. We launched over one hundred of these recently. These are mainstream cricket clubs that want to make their clubs more accessible to people with disabilities. The aim is to increase this number to 300 by 2025 in the United Kingdom.

As part of this programme, clubs can receive some adaptive kits, disability awareness training and other things to make the club more accessible.

Looking at coaching more generally, it's worth noting that a good coach is a good coach across the board. They can communicate well, they can adapt their sessions and style based on the audience they're working with and they can understand who they're coaching and work well accordingly. This doesn't change with people with disabilities. It's about working with what the player does have and adapt accordingly.

There are different pathways for players looking to progress, based on their disabilities. In a general sense, it's about playing the highest standard of cricket you possibly can. More information on the pathways for each disability is available from the ECB.

ISA GUHA – BROADCASTER AND FORMER ENGLAND CRICKETER

Educate yourself. I think the word education is thrown around a lot, but until there is a willingness to learn about different people's backgrounds and cultures, you can never understand what people are going through or be aware of it.

CHAPTER SUMMARY

- There's a lot of work on EDI being done by some incredibly inspirational people, listen carefully to their advice to make sure your club is entirely inclusive
- Clubs should be proactive in recruiting players from *all* backgrounds
- Create opportunities for players and volunteers of all ages
- Incorporate a very clear feedback loop within your organisation
- Cricket (and sport in general) plays an enormous role in improving society
- Make sure individuals can express clearly what their needs are

CHAPTER 9

Advice for Players

I wanted to finish the book with a chapter aimed squarely at the most important people the book aims to help.

Female players.

The greatest gift that we as former players, current players, coaches, volunteers, administrators and cricket enthusiasts can bring to the game that has given us so much is to give back as much advice and support to the next generation as we possibly can.

Below is a collection of snippets of knowledge from those who know the game best.

I'd love it if you shared these with any female players you might know or work with (and male players too!).

Isa Guha, Broadcaster and Former England Cricketer

I think trying to absorb as much information as possible is good initially because then you can work out what works for you or not. It's important to try things and know that it's a journey; you don't have to have all of the answers, and every step is a learning step whether you've won or lost or have a good or bad training session – it's all a learning experience to grow as a player.

Georgia Adams, Professional Cricketer

Take every opportunity you can to watch or play the game; this will be the most valuable learning experience on offer as a young cricketer.

Training smart and practicing skills is incredibly important, but time spent in the middle is something I found to be instrumental in my growth as a player, as you learn so much from players around you and it's about developing a mindset to execute skills practiced in training when you are out on the pitch.

Fundamentally, above all, work hard, enjoy what you do and keep reaching for your goals as you never know what opportunities may be around the corner.

Lisa Sthalekar, Broadcaster and Former Australian Cricketer

My main advice is that you have to love what you do and be passionate about it, because if you are, you will be willing to do all the little things.

Unfortunately, if you want to make it to the top you have to make little sacrifices along the way. First might be missing out on friends' parties, watching what you eat, doing a session even when you are tired and, more importantly, doing the sometimes boring drills over and over again. At the end of the day, it's all worth it!

When learning a new skill, I try and go right back to basics, so for instance if I am learning a pull shot. I might use tennis balls and get someone to lob the ball on the full in the perfect position to execute the shot. I may even begin in the final position, so all I need to do is swing through the shot. I would then slowly go back to normal batting stance, but still getting them to lob the ball on the full to me. Once I had mastered that in a closed environment, I would then ask my partner to go back a bit and bounce the ball so that it again comes up to the height that I need it to. Again once I have mastered it, then the speed would increase.

Fran Wilson, Professional Cricketer and Former England Player

Have a forward-thinking mindset. Don't dwell on mistakes or bad days; they can impact your enjoyment and therefore your learning. Try to learn to move on and look forward to the next game or training session.

Alex Hartley, Professional Cricketer and Broadcaster

Enjoyment is key, never forget why you started the game! You start because you love it, never lose that love as tough as sessions or seasons can be.

The harder you work and the more time you put into something, the more you will see the reward; it may take time, but it's worth it in the end.

Never feel frightened to ask for advice no matter who you are talking to or who you are training with; you can often learn more from your teammates than anyone else.

Suzie Bates, New Zealand Cricketer

Being a captain can be one of the most enjoyable and also challenging roles in a team. My first piece of advice is to do it your way and stay true to yourself. Lots of people will want to have their say and input which is great, but your job is to sift through all of that info to make decisions you are happy with and committed to – it's important to remember these decisions don't always have to be the right ones; they just have to be your ones.

When you first start in the role, it is easy to be preoccupied with making the 'right' decision all the time which can sometimes delay your decision-making process or cloud it when you have a lot of external input. The key is accepting we are never going to make the right decisions all the time, but as long as you are committed to what you are doing and can explain the thinking behind your decisions, that is a great start.

Lastly, it is a role you will grow into; there isn't a manual as to what your captaincy journey should look like – and you won't get it right from the start. My main advice is to remember the times when things have worked well then learn from and embrace those times when they haven't gone you're way; our mistakes are often our best tools for learning.

Jenny Gunn MBE, Professional Cricketer and Former England Cricketer

Athletic: if you put the hard work in off the field, you will be able to play harder on the field. Hit the ball further and bowl for longer, but it takes time to get cricket fit. Don't be afraid to get down on the floor diving and rolling around. The more you get used to it, the more you will take your chance in a game.

Smart: learning from others and watching to gain little insights for your own game. Asking questions will only help you in the future. Learning bowling angles, when you bowl certain balls, which boundary/bowler to target, weaker fielder and so on. You never stop learning.

All-round game: even if you're not an all-rounder, realise that you can make an impact in other areas. If you're not a batter, work on a shot where you can get a single to get off strike or a boundary option if required. Also realise that you can have a massive impact in the field.

But don't forget to have fun as this is when we play at our best!

Alyssa Healey, Australian Cricketer

My first piece of advice for any budding wicketkeeper would be to spend time developing the basic skills. This doesn't have to be in a formal environment; it could be playing other sports – playing catch with a friend or simply going through a series of footwork drills at a local park.

At training try to set aside ten minutes at the start or end of your session to work on your catching technique. Here is a nice routine to get lots of catches – ask a partner to underarm the catches from 5 meters away:

20 catches with two hands
20 catches to your left (left hand only)
20 catches to your right (right hand only)
20 catches with two hands

Try to keep nice and low with your knees bent and weight forward when taking the catches.

Lastly, enjoy it! As wicketkeepers, we're in the game every single ball so we will make mistakes, but it's really important you put those mistakes to one side so you can focus on the next ball – that next ball could be when you produce a match-winning stumping or catch behind! In a nutshell, our job is to simply watch and catch the ball – remember to watch the ball all the way in and you will be fine!

Amy Jones, England Cricketer

As a wicketkeeper, it's important to feel fully involved in every ball of the innings. It's also important to think bravely. In the modern game with players often moving around the crease, you need to hold your shape and watch the ball into your hands no matter what the batter does.

If a mistake happens, park it and get yourself in the mindset of catching the next one.

Katherine Brunt, England Cricketer

As a bowler, I like to have only three or four variations and work hard to get really good at them. If I had too many of them, there's less time to do them as well. I work on the off-cutter, the one from the back of my hand, the yorker and the bouncer

Laura Marsh, Coach and Former England Cricketer

I became an off spinner simply by trying different things in the nets. I used to primarily bowl seam and then tried some leg spin and a bit of off spin. One of the coaches noticed I had some talent as an off spinner, so I stuck with it.

My advice to players who'd like to spin the ball more would be to have an attitude to it! Put it in your mind to spin it hard, then work the skill aspect of it from there.

Nat Sciver, England Cricketer

Don't forget to develop a pre-match routine. I like to arrive early and have one of the coaches throw some underarms at me to get my head towards the ball and get my weight transferred towards the ball.

When I start my innings I like to concentrate on hitting the ball straight, then expand on this as the innings progress and I feel more 'in'.

Lisa Keightley, Head Coach of England and Former Australian Cricketer

Most players who make it are pretty resilient. You have so many ups and downs in cricket through form, through life and through environments.

I think these are the three things you have to juggle. You have to juggle environments because not every environment is going to suit you. You need to work out how you're going to get the best out of yourself in that environment. I think form, you go up and down because you're learning. If you look at Nat Sciver, she had a brilliant 12 months, followed by a blip in form for a short while. To be resilient, you still need to have confidence and belief that 'you know what, I'm just going through a little rough patch'. Usually, there are a couple of things you struggle with. So for some, it might be fitness. It could be speed. It could be one of your three skills: batting, bowling and fielding. You're going to struggle in all three at some stage. But it's how you deal with that struggle. If you've got good mentors, or good parents, or teachers or a coach that you worked with, you can talk to outside some of those environments. It really helps if you've got some cool people. And parents are a huge support. Don't put too much pressure on kids or know how to talk to them consistently on good days and bad days. Your parents can really help you through. You'll always have one coach who you really gel with and you can talk to, and then just have fun with your mates.

Ebony Rainford-Brent – Broadcaster and Former England Cricketer

The growth mindset is the most important thing for you if you want to reach higher levels. Always learn, always develop. Learn to enjoy the process of growth and improvement. If I could have been a little more relaxed and growth focussed during my career, I could have accelerated it even more.

Courtney Winfield-Hill, Coach

Remember, success can be so many things. Not everyone who plays will play international cricket or win a World Cup. Say 'YES!' to as many opportunities the game offers you and utilise these to develop your character. Our game is a terrific builder of character! This then becomes transferable to all you do within and away from cricket. Now to me, that's true success.

Heather Knight OBE, England Captain

If you're looking to make it to the higher levels of the game, you'll have to go through a few setbacks and a few things that don't quite go right. Being able to come back from those is really important. I've always had the desire to want to make it to the top, and that's always what drove me, drove training and drove me wanting to be a better cricketer.

Enjoyment as well is really important; enjoying the process of trying to get better and playing is super important. There have definitely been times when I've taken myself a bit too seriously, and I've learned as I've got older and more experienced, that it's almost better not to overthink things and not to take things too seriously at times.

Making sure you've done all your work, and you relax when you do play, I think that's really important. A lot of young girls put so much pressure on themselves that it can affect their performance. If you train hard, you can be more relaxed when playing.

Looking after the confidence became important for me, I've learned to do a lot more as I've developed and seen the bigger picture, not just focussing on one bad game; that's really important for me now.

I try and always be quite consistent in how I am, whether we're winning or losing, and how I am on the pitch. I think it's quite important to stay level as a captain, not always giving too much away. You're the person that people look to when things are going wrong, and so if you're generally quite level, that can be a good calming influence.

Making a bad decision is better than making no decision. I think that's something I've tried to always stick to. I make sure that I actually make a decision, commit to it and go with it fully rather than not making a decision and letting things go by.

Try and be clear with players in your instructions, bowlers in particular. Try and go back to a simple plan if things aren't going well, and keep it really simple. What you're going to bowl, okay, great. We'll set the feel for that, go commit to it and execute. Simplicity is often key, I think. I think there's always a tendency to try and overcomplicate things, so keeping things as simple as possible under pressure is really important.

Clare Connor CBE, Sports Administrator and Former England Captain

Try to understand *yourself* better; it's from there that you make all decisions. Whether it's a small decision like a shot selection or a much bigger and more significant one.

Understanding yourself is so important. Engage in the mental side of sport; however, don't do it to such an extent that you lose your natural sense of self and your love for the game.

I always liked the quote 'If you can't lead yourself, you can't lead others'.

Be curious about yourself. To understand your weaknesses is not a weakness, it's a sign of strength.

Hannah Stobbs, Cricket for Girls Coach

What have I learned? The things that I told my younger self that I was not good at fielding and batting are the very things that I enjoy the most while playing cricket for my current club, Ickenham CC. Once a shy, overly competitive and serious bowler, now an outgoing, fun-loving opening batter who isn't afraid to use her hands to field the ball and take the odd catch when required. Growing up, I would put pressure on myself to perform, filled with worry about making mistakes and letting my team down. Now I walk onto the field with a smile on my face and a sense of gratitude that I can play cricket with some of my closest friends. In the more challenging moments such as the battles in our head and the injury setbacks, it's the people who we surround ourselves with who carry us through and empower us to build stronger, longer lasting foundations for future success.

My advice to players: Know that your contributions are valuable; know that you can impact pressure situations on a cricket field by small, yet meaningful actions; know that you are important and your team values you. You are a remarkable human first and a cricketer second. It is from that space that you will thrive and perform to the best of your ability. Go well.

Kate Cross, England Cricketer

- Enjoy the game and everything it gives you. Whether it's competitiveness, friendship, travel or fun. There was a reason you started playing cricket in the first place and it's important to keep that motivation throughout your journey.
- Do the hard bits. Whether it's skill, fitness, nutrition or even looking after your mental health, make sure you do it. Being able to step out onto the pitch with the comfort that you have done everything to be in the best place possible will always stand you in better stead.
- Be clear. I've played my best cricket when I have been super clear on what I am trying to execute. Whether that is being at the top of my run up and having clarity on the ball I am going to try and execute, or whether it's knowing what my role for the team is. Being clear can sometimes take away a lot of the 'clutter' that cricket can sometimes create.

One of the recurring themes throughout these snippets is the concept of enjoyment. Ultimately, we want all young girls and women to have full access to the game, so they have the opportunity to enjoy all the benefits it can give us. I sincerely hope this book has helped in some way to contribute towards this.

If we want to grow the game as we do, the only way we can do it is together.

Thanks for reading.

CHAPTER SUMMARY

- Everything you do is a learning experience, good or bad!
- Enjoyment is key
- Always ask for advice
- Put the hard work in off the field
- Develop the basic skills really well
- Try different things
- Have a growth mindset
- Understand *yourself*

Glossary of Terms

APPEAL

The bowler will appeal to the umpire by shouting 'howzat?!' as a way of asking the umpire if the batter is out. This is used for LBW and caught-behind decisions that aren't always as clear as other dismissals; hence the umpire needs to be asked to make the decision.

EXTRA

Runs not scored by the batter. There are four common extras – byes, leg byes, wides and no balls. In Australia, these are known as sundries.

FULL TOSS

A ball that reaches the batter without bouncing. Above waist height, it becomes a beamer.

GOOD LENGTH DELIVERY

The ideal length that the bowler aims for, getting the batter in two minds as whether to play forward or back.

HALF VOLLEY

A ball that is the perfect length for driving, fuller than a good length but not a full toss.

INNINGS

In its simplest form, an innings is when one team completes their batting go (either by using up all the overs or being bowled out). The second innings is when the team batting second completes their batting go. Most games are split into two innings – similar to halves in football or hockey.

LBW

A method by which a batter is dismissed and is one of the more complex part of the game. Meaning 'leg before wicket', and in basic form, the ball hits the batter on their pads and if the umpire deems that the ball would have gone on to hit the stumps then the decision of out will be made.

LEG BYE

When the ball deflects off the pad and the batter run. A shot must be offered to the ball. Leg byes do not count against the bowler.

BEAMER

A ball that does not bounce (usually accidentally) and passes the batter at or about head height. If aimed straight at the batter by a fast bowler, this is a very dangerous delivery (and generally frowned on).

BOUNCER

A short-pitched ball that passes the batter at chest or head height (also known as a 'bumper').

BOUNDARY

The perimeter of a cricket field often marked with a white line, rope or individual markers such as cones. Also, the act of the batter scoring a four or a six (e.g., 'Heather Knight hammered three boundaries in a row').

BYE

A run scored when the batter does not touch the ball with either their bat or body. A bye happens most often when the wicketkeeper misses the ball which therefore allows the batters enough time to complete one run or more.

CREASE

The area of the wicket which dictates where the batters stand and also helps umpires make decisions with regard to stumpings and run-outs.

DUCK

A score of zero by a batter.

cricketforgirls.com – the online resource library providing you with the confidence and knowledge to deliver a full programme of cricket. © 2019 Cricket for Girls Ltd.

LEG SPIN

A type of bowling that spins away from the right-hander after it bounces – from leg to off stump (from right to left). Also known as wrist spin.

MAIDEN

A completed over where no runs are scored off the bat.

MANKAD

Mankad is when the bowler brings their arm round and, instead of releasing the ball, runs out the non-striker by whipping off the bails. This type of dismissal is rare – usually, a warning is given to the batter beforehand. This is also considered to be against the 'Spirit of Cricket'. (Named after Vinoo Mankad, who twice dismissed the Australian Bill Brown this way.)

MCC

The Marylebone Cricket Club, the spiritual home of cricket at Lord's in St Johns Wood in London. It was founded in 1787, the autocratic arbiter in cricket matters, and no law could be changed without its approval. While the administration of the game worldwide has moved to the International Cricket Council, and to the England and Wales Cricket Board in Britain, the MCC is still regarded as the ultimate defender of the laws of the game, a type of Privy Council of cricket.

NICK

A faint edge off the bat.

NO BALL

An illegitimate delivery, usually when the bowler has overstepped on the front crease, bowled a beamer or bowled a ball that bounces more than once (at performance level) or more than twice (at recreational level). This particular rule can vary depending on which format of cricket is being played.

OFF SPIN

A type of bowling that spins into the right-hander after it bounces – from off to leg stump (from left to right). Also known as finger spin.

OUT

There are ten possible ways of being out: bowled, caught, hit wicket, lbw, stumped, timed out, obstruction, hit the ball twice and run out. To be out 'retired out' is gaining in currency and popularity and counts as a dismissal, unlike 'retired hurt'.

OVER

Innings are made up of a number of overs. Each over is made up of six deliveries being bowled by one bowler in a row.

SLEDGING

The act of verbally abusing or unsettling a batter, in an attempt to make them lose concentration and give his wicket away. Often offensive, occasionally amusing, and always a topic of conversation.

WICKET MAIDEN

The same as a maiden, although with the addition of the bowler taking a wicket.

WIDE

A delivery that pitches too far away for the batter to hit. The umpire will single this by stretching their arms out horizontally, an extra will be added to the total, and the ball will be bowled again.

YORKER

A full-pitched delivery that is aimed at the batter's toes and/or the base of the stumps. A type of ball bowlers try to bowl towards the end of the batting innings to restrict them from scoring.